A FERMANAGH CHILDHOOD

D1599918

From Dorothy

To Dorothy

Have Good Reading

Feb 1989.

The Friar's Bush Press gratefully acknowledges the
generous support of the Fermanagh District Council

The Friar's Bush Press
24 College Park Ave
Belfast BT7 1LR
1988

Front cover painted by Denise Ferran.
Printed by W & G Baird Antrim.

A
Fermanagh childhood

by

William K. Parke

FRIAR'S BUSH PRESS

Contents

The author with his mother, father, sister Elsie and his dog Toby,
c. 1933.

1 Early Days

IN THE HEART of the Fermanagh Lakeland nestles the little village of Derrygonnelly, ten miles from the county town of Enniskillen. Few people outside the county have ever heard of the place, for nothing out of the ordinary has ever happened there – no historical battles fought in the area, no well-known landmarks, no famous people came from there and any local scandal, likely to bring adverse publicity, was kept strictly under wraps and confined to the natives.

The village, of just over five hundred souls, is situated in drumlin country about three miles south of Lower Lough Erne and is surrounded by green hills, heathy mountains, bogs and rocky pastures. Little lakes pepper the countryside, many of them containing crannogs, those mysterious little islands made by the lake dwellers of long ago. Streams of pure spring water feed these little lakes and then larger streams flow out either into Lough Erne or into the main river of the area known as the Sillees.

If you can find Derrygonnelly on the map you will see that it is situated on the banks of the Sillees river. If you look more closely you will see that the river flows almost parallel to Lower Lough Erne but in the opposite direction, so it appears to flow against the hill. Does it really flow against the hill? To throw some light on this phenomenon we go back over a thousand years when we had in this area a lady saint. Some people might say that few females are saints but we definitely had a lady saint known as Saint Faber and, accompanied by her pet deer, she roamed the area endeavouring to convert the locals to Christianity. Whether she met with much success or not, we do not know, but like most ambitious women she decided to start at the top, and her main objective was a local

Chieftain, O'Phelan. His castle was built into the limestone rocks at Killydrum.

The story goes that O'Phelan, on seeing the lady and her pet deer approach, decided that he wanted nothing to do with this new fangled religion; he would stand by his old Druid friends who had served him and his ancestors for hundreds of years and who could cure any ailment in man or beast and cast eerie spells on his enemies. Perhaps he was just allergic to lady saints or, worse still, to women in general. Whatever the reason, he ordered his servants to release his hunting dogs on this unfortunate girl as she and her pet deer approached his rocky stronghold. St Faber fled for her life and attempted to jump the river which lay in her path. Alas! She was not an athlete: both she and her deer landed in the middle of the river, destroying her holy books. She struggled to the opposite bank, wet, cold and angry. No 'turning the other cheek' for St Faber; she cast a spell on O'Phelan's castle and caused it to disappear into a hole in the rocks. She wasn't finished there; she cast three curses on the river whose only crime was to be in the wrong place at the wrong time. The curses were that the river was to be dangerous for bathers, bad for fishing and to flow for ever against the hill.

Ever since, this seemingly harmless little river has claimed many victims. You could fish from its banks for hours and not get so much as a nibble, and after heavy rain, which happens all too often in this part of Ireland, hundreds of acres are flooded. There have been many drainage schemes over the years, without success. St Faber reigns supreme and O'Phelan has a lot to answer for in lost revenue to local farmers.

There is one half mile stretch of the Sillees river where there is a good fall and it was here that our ancestors chose to found the little community called Derrygonnelly. It was a wise move on the part of our ancestors because the river meant a constant water supply for both man and beast. The swift flow at that point meant that effluent from the village was washed away thus preventing outbreaks of cholera and fever which were very prevalent in the days before sewage systems.

For many years the cluster of houses along the banks of the river could only be described as a hamlet, but in the late eighteenth century a village began to develop and so eventually we had a street about two hundred yards long with a population of around two hundred souls living in sixty houses of various shapes and sizes.

The nearest town, ten miles away, is the county town of Enniskillen and to the west lie the villages of Belleek and Garrison. Lough Erne lies about three miles to the north and to the south there is a mixture of pasture, rocks, mountains and bogs.

Today many giant passenger aircraft pass over our village on their way from Britain to America. On a clear day, as the passengers gaze down at this little village nestling between the mountains and Lough Erne, do they give us a second thought; do they wonder if we still keep pigs in the kitchen?

Derrygonnelly is truly an isolated village situated on a road to nowhere. No matter what village or hamlets travellers want to visit, they can travel directly to their destination without passing through our village. The Department of the Environment erects signposts directing strangers and tourists to our many beauty spots but these signs seem to give our village a miss. I've often wondered why.

This is the village where I was born and brought up and this is where I have spent most of my life. Now that I am in my sixties I can reflect on that life and I must confess it was a grand wee place in which to grow up and live. I was born the year of the General Strike and brought up during the years of the depression. If a psychologist ever gets the chance to probe my mind, I'm sure he will blame this background for my many deficiencies!

Lower Main Street, Derrygonnelly in the early 1930s.

2   First Memories

A CRISP NORTH WIND was blowing on a cold January afternoon. At precisely three o'clock in the afternoon, just as the children were coming out of school, I first saw the light of day, in the year of 1926. I was born in the same house, indeed the same bedroom as my father, and my grandfather was born in the house next door; both houses being on the village street. I was the youngest of five children, indeed I was described as a 'little late one', perhaps an accident. My sister who is twelve years older informed me recently, while reminiscing, that 'I was not a welcome guest' when I arrived – perhaps not in her eyes as she would be expected to look after me. Maybe I was an accident for my mother was forty two years old and my father forty nine when I was born. In spite of these obstacles I arrived safely and in good health and was always loved by both of them. I often heard my mother tell young expectant mothers by way of encouragement that she would rather have a baby than have a tooth extracted. It didn't say much for the dentists of sixty years ago. She took childbearing in her stride as most women did in those days; no ante natal clinics, no breathing exercises or rolling around the floor for hours on end.

My mother simply set the fire in the bedroom ready to light when zero hour approached. In the meantime she carried on with her usual work in the kitchen or behind the counter in the shop. Before my birth, around midday the tell-tale signs were felt, so up she went to the bedroom and lit the fire while my father sent for Dr McSorley and the midwife, Mrs Busby. Eventually I arrived safe and sound and after a few days my mother was back serving behind the counter. My brothers Ernie and Harry and sister Flo arrived home from school and were conducted upstairs to see their newly arrived red-haired

5

brother who had just been found under a cabbage head in the garden and was now warmly wrapped in a cradle. I was told that Harry looked into the cradle and said 'we will call him Willie' and so they did. Ever since I have been called Willie, William, Bill, Billy and Ginger.

Some weeks later I was baptised William Kittson Parke, the Kittson being my mother's maiden name. The baptismal service did not take place in the local church as it was three miles away and the weather was much too cold to transport a small child by pony and trap; instead I was baptised at evening service in the local Orange Hall. There was no baptismal font; instead, the hall caretaker, Davis, produced a porridge bowl containing pure spring water and the ceremony took place. Just imagine! Baptised in an Orange Hall!

My sister Elsie was a couple of years older than me and sister Flo, who was twelve years older, more or less reared her and was devoted to her. My arrival upset matters slightly as the novelty of small children in the home had begun to wear thin as far as Flo was concerned and she didn't look forward to starting all over again. However, with the efforts of my mother and father, together with the maid, shop assistants and yardmen, I was reared with great care, love and affection.

Naturally I don't remember the early part of my life but I have early recollections of being bathed in an oval-shaped, galvanized bathpan in front of a large black Carron kitchen range. There was no piped supply of water in the village at the time and therefore no bathrooms or flush toilets. Water was carried in buckets from the river or from water barrels, which caught the rainwater from the roofs of the buildings. It was then boiled in large black metal pots and kettles on the range and poured into the bath. This unwieldy process meant that your bathing was cut to a minimum. There were many people in the neighbourhood who never had a bath since their youth, apart from the odd rub down on the banks of a stream. Drinking water was drawn from several springs around the village but during a dry spell in the summer the water supply could be a serious problem. Spring wells went low, the river was reduced to a slimy trickle and the water barrels ran dry.

Some people had a bath once a year; they went to the seaside resort of Bundoran, where there was a gentleman who ran an establishment in which you could have a bath in fresh water, sea water, cold or hot, or a seaweed bath for one shilling, which kept you refreshed for the next twelve months. No-one knew the meaning of 'B.O.' and you could tell what a person did for a living by their smell. Children were bathed either in wooden tubs or galvanized bathpans. The vessels were also used for washing clothes and when pigs were being slaughtered they were used in the scalding process when shaving the hair off the carcass. A local old timer who moved recently into a modern pensioner's bungalow informed me that he had no intention of having a bath. The last bath he had was over fifty years ago in Bundoran. It opened his pores to such an extent that he developed severe pains in his joints which lasted for months and that taught him a lesson he never forgot.

Another of my early fleeting recollections is of sitting in some kind of high chair in the kitchen. Nowadays the focal point of the home is the living-room but in my early days it was the kitchen; the term 'living-room' was unheard of. Here you ate, cooked, prepared the food, ironed the clothes, sat, chatted and entertained the callers. Small children were put in a wooden cradle beside the fire and rocked to sleep. The woman of the house could rock the cradle with her foot, mend clothes, knit or stir the porridge and chat, all at the same time. There were no walkie pens or playpens. A very small child was often put in the horse's collar on a blanket on the kitchen floor. In farm houses the horse's collar was usually hung on the kitchen wall so that the lining and padding were kept dry. You could hardly find a more comfortable or safe place for a small baby than inside a horse's collar.

Every home had a wooden cradle on rockers. Our cradle was made up by old James the cooper, who lived just outside the village. It was made for my eldest brother who was born in 1912 and was used by all five of us, ending with yours truly, fourteen years later. I don't remember being in it but I do remember the cradle being used by my elder sister for her doll. When my mother was sure there were going to be no more babies she gave the cradle to a young mother in the village. Later when a child could stand, the playpen was a tea chest and sometimes a child, who was inclined to crawl, was put under an upturned turf creel. Today we have carrycots, playpens and walkie pens but are they an improvement on the horse's collar, the cradle, the tea chest or even the upturned turf creel? Are the babies any happier?

The rich people had prams; the others just carried the child around on their hip or it was looked after by an elder brother or sister. Children received few toys and were clothed in home-made clothes, which were handed down. They learned to amuse themselves, were taught at an early age to do chores around the home and, most important of all, they received an immense amount of love and devotion and were nourished on plain, home-produced food.

The kitchen was where the ceilidhers were entertained, exchanging news and gossip, and telling stories; even a good liar was a source of entertainment and the advent of the gramophone was a great boon. In our kitchen we had a bench or couch in the corner next to the range; to the other side of the old couch stood the dresser where the crockery and cutlery were kept on the top half, while underneath were two presses containing cooking pots and supplies. The crockery ranged from pint mugs to china cups. There were two tables which were scrubbed white every day; one for preparing the food and the other where we ate, together with an assortment of wooden chairs and stools. The four-legged and three-legged stools were useful and they were stored underneath the tables when not in use. Bacon and plum puddings were hung from hooks on the ceiling, next to the wet clothes suspended from clothes lines on pulleys. It was remarkable how much happened in the kitchen which always seemed to be congested with cooking, washing, utensils of all kinds and callers.

The old black range fairly devoured coal in order to keep the big ovens going, providing heat, cooking for a large number of hungry mouths of between twelve and fifteen persons daily, and drying wet clothes as well as being the focal point of both activity and inactivity. It was lovingly cleaned out and black-leaded daily. Before the installation of this monster, a plain hearth fire and a crane crook sufficed for my grandfather and grandmother who reared eleven children in this house. How did they cook for so many on a turf hearth fire? I don't imagine they had six course meals.

The inhabitants of the village were one big family. You could see from the top end what was going on at the lower end. If you had hefty lungs you could call or whistle in order to attract a person's attention from one end of the village to the other. As small children or even toddlers we wandered quite safely up and down the one street. A mother kept an eye on all children in the vicinity of her home as well as her own. Children wandered into any house, sat down at the fire and ate a slice of bread, often with a little sugar sprinkled on it. Although children had free run of the village, two things were engrained on their minds from an early age. One was 'Keep away from the river, especially when it is in flood'. St Faber was held in great respect. The other was, 'Don't cross the street on your own'. Why be so careful crossing the street of our little village, when you saw one motor car once a week? There was quite a volume of heavy horsedrawn traffic, especially in the forenoons, and also ponies and spring carts and asses and carts. You just cannot jam on the brakes when driving a spirited horse or swerve in and out to avoid a child. When I was a boy I had several pet dogs who were run over by horse carts: I never had one killed by a car.

There was no such thing as National dried milk for babies or any other kind of dried milk or babyfood. A child was nursed by its mother and then weaned on to cows' or goats' milk. Tuberculosis or consumption was rampant and took a heavy toll especially among the young. Everyone was poor, many desperately poor, but I never heard anyone complain or say they were poor. Deep down they knew there was no way out and they were content with their lot in life and, on the whole, were very happy. Luxuries were non-existent and their needs were simple.

Mill School, Derrygonnelly, 1933. The author is in the top row, second from the end on the right.

3 School

WHEN CHILDREN reached the age of six they went to school. If they had to walk a long distance they might wait until they were almost seven. I lived only one hundred yards or so from the school so I went when I was five and a half. Our school was known as Derrygonnelly Mill Public Elementary School. The word Mill originated from the old school beside the scutch mill which our school replaced. The school building consisted of two schoolrooms (the big room and the 'wee' room) and a porch for hanging coats, with a little fuel store at one end; that was the entire school building. Outside there was a small muddy playground for the boys and another for the girls. At the bottom of each were toilets, which were cleaned out once a year during the summer holidays. What a health hazard! Each child brought a shilling each year to cover the cost of fuel for the winter months. We also had to buy our own books, which was a great burden on poor families when wages were about fifteen shillings a week and often less. There were no school meals; each child brought lunch, usually bread and butter, whilst some lucky children had jam and occasionally allowed others to share their good fortune by rubbing the slices together.

There were between sixty and seventy pupils at the school and they were taught in the two small classrooms by the two teachers. The pupils were graded into eight classes from junior infants to sixth class. There was not enough room for all the children to sit at any one time so in each room two classes stood while two sat. The classes standing did reading, spelling, geography and scripture, while those sitting did composition, dictation and grammar. Those who stood did so in a complete semi-circle either around the fireplace or around a

11

map. There was a semi-circular figure of brass studs in the floor and dare you put your foot inside! We stood with the intelligent pupils at the head of the class right down to the dunces at the bottom, a system not designed to instil confidence. Strange as it may sound, looking back, most of those at the bottom of the classes did fairly well; indeed a few did exceptionally well and none of those at the top made much of a mark that I can recall! If through boredom your mind wandered slightly and you inadvertently put a foot inside the brass studs a sharp thump on the shin from the Master's pointer brought you back to life or maybe he just stood on your toes.

After each period those standing sat down and those sitting placed themselves behind the brass studs.

The pupils stayed at school until they were fourteen years old and every pupil looked forward for years to their fourteenth birthday. Our two teachers were Mr and Mrs Kingston; two opposites. Old Kingston, as he was known throughout the community, was extremely cross, often vicious and sadistic, while his wife was a very kind serene lady; she soon retired and her daughter, also a very kind person, took over as assistant. We were happy and considered ourselves safe in the junior 'wee' room, but when we graduated to the Master's room life changed from happiness to misery. We were 'slapped' with a cane or a pointer on the fingers for the least misdemeanour, wrong spelling, untidy work, lateness for school, talking in class, giving an incorrect answer to a question, or dumb insolence; the list could go on. Sometimes we received one 'slap', other times perhaps four of five. We even received slaps and didn't know what they were for. Our fingers were first very painful and then became quite numb. Often when we arrived home our parents asked us 'How many slaps did you get today?', but there was no sympathy forthcoming.

Mr Kingston was of course responsible for the entire school and taught four classes under crowded conditions. We were taught the first eighteen theorems of Euclid, algebra up to equations and also Latin roots. There were pupils who were slow to grasp all he tried to teach them; those who were not blessed with average intelligence were sadly left behind as there were no facilities or time for backward children.

I remember brief glimpses of my first days at school. The first school book contained pictures and words – man, saw, cat, mat, rat and then short sentences – 'The cat is on the mat', 'I saw the man'. The next school book was slightly more advanced 'Rex is a big dog, he is six; he is as old as I am'. I remember sitting in the little desks in the 'wee' room writing and drawing on our slates with chalk, playing with plasticine or listening to Mrs Kingston reading us stories. How we loved story time! Learning nursery rhymes, chanting the two times, three times, and four times tables, spelling simple words, all singing or chanting together so that you never forgot it until your dying breath – a form of brainwashing. We could hear the Master in the big room shouting at the pupils; we could hear the cane go swish as some poor unfortunates received their quota of slaps or maybe a few cracks on the knuckles. We did not look forward to our graduation to the third class. Sometimes the punishment was quite silent as you were dragged by the short hair on your temples to the blackboard where you were humiliated in front of the entire classroom, absolutely petrified and convinced that you were as stupid as an ass.

The locals, those who were lucky enough to have left school, used to tell us 'He's a good teacher, for he'd knock the "larnin" into you'. In fact, the majority of Old Kingston's pupils can look back and admit that he was a good teacher, although it did not seem like it at the time.

We read *Lorna Doone, The Merchant of Venice, The Wind in the Willows* and *Ivanhoe*. The Master really had an obsession with English grammar. I suppose it never crossed his mind as to how grammar was going to benefit boys and girls who were destined to end up on the farm, or as maids, labourers and shop assistants, for few made the big time either in business or the professions and we all spoke in our native dialect of which I have always been proud. We had indicative and subjunctive mood, we had conjunctions, interjections, participles and prepositions, regular verbs, adjectives, adverbs, case and tense. We had nouns and a vast number of pronouns; personal, possessive, relative, demonstrative and, the old faithful, the indefinite; 'any, all, few, some, several, one, other, another, none'. I never forgot the indefinite pronouns and many a time when I had to listen to people who insisted on demonstrating their knowledge of Shakespeare or reciting the works of famous poets, I would chime in at an opportune moment by relating the indefinite pronouns. No-one ever knew what I was talking about but they did catch on that I was making fun. To this day, however, my grammar is bad and my spelling atrocious, but, who knows, they could be worse only for Old Kingston.

For our geography we were required to rhyme off the counties of the four provinces of Ireland, the main towns of each county and the industries for which each was noted. It would be difficult to rhyme off what main towns are noted for today; most of the old established industries are long gone to be replaced by those that are here today and gone tomorrow. The main rivers, lakes, bays and mountains were also drummed into our little heads together with a wide knowledge of the geography of the British Isles and Europe, together with their populations.

We had singing for one period in the week; part of this period was spent singing the tonic solfa, doh, ray, me, fa, so, la, te, doh. We also sang old Irish favourites such as *The ash grove, The meeting of the waters* and the negro spirituals, *Poor old Joe* and *Polly Wolly Doodle.* Friday was poetry day when we learned to recite the old faithfuls – *The village blacksmith, The boy stood on the burning deck, Lucy Grey, The charge of the Light Brigade* and many others that are no longer in print and long forgotten.

Scripture was taught in the first period every day and to a strict syllabus. We learned off by heart, a catechism, psalms and long passages of scripture. Nevertheless, scripture was one of our favourite subjects, probably because of the beautiful stories in the Bible. I was fortunate for we had in our home, during my formative years, a maid named Annie. Annie had little education but she was very intelligent and a born teacher. Her father died when she was very young and her mother was left to rear a young family as best she could. In this day and age of free education she would have gone far in that profession. Instead she left her little country school at the age of fourteen and soon went into service. Nevertheless, Annie went about her work without complaint and was always pleasant. Every night she watched over my sister and me while we were struggling with our homework, spellings, reading, poetry and, of course, the confounded grammar. But Annie really excelled teaching us our scripture, for she was a devout Roman Catholic and really lived up to the Christian faith. Learning catechism is extremely boring for a child no matter what their religion, but Annie managed to bring more meaning and life into the Church of Ireland catechism than I ever experienced before ör since. When teaching us the psalms or portions of scripture she read them with her gentle, quiet voice and she had that rare gift of portraying the beauty of the words with great feeling. In the morning, just as we were about to leave for school, Annie usually appeared from the scullery sink; 'Come on into the room, children, and we will go over your spellings and scripture once more'. Annie received her true calling when a few years later she entered a convent. She joined a French order and spent the war years in occupied France. Few of us manage to live up to the teachings of the Scriptures but Annie's early teaching and example left a lasting impression with me.

The only recreation which we had was a half hour break for lunch and play; no morning or afternoon breaks. Sports facilities were non-existent. There wasn't even a football. There were two small muddy playgrounds – one for the girls and the other for the boys. I don't know why we were separated but we didn't dare wander into the wrong playground!

If pupils missed a day at school they were closely questioned the following day as to why they were absent. The Master seemed to be able to penetrate the mind as to whether the excuse was genuine. If he was satisfied, well and good: if not then the unfortunate pupils found themselves with numb fingers, a one day absence especially was looked upon with suspicion. Most of the excuses were sickness; pains in the tummy or head. Helping at home on the farm was not tolerated as an excuse. One girl's excuse was, 'Please Sir, the mare died', and another was 'The sow was pigging'. The mare dying would have been a catastrophe on a small farm and if the sow had a good litter, at least nine or ten piglets, it was a cause for rejoicing. Either of these events were of the utmost significance on a farm but not to our teacher.

Although we had two schools of different denominations in the village, all the children played together in the evenings and during the school holidays. It was difficult for small children, who happily played together, to understand why they should attend separate schools, churches and even places of entertainment, but thankfully community relations have always been excellent. Over the years when any degree of discord entered our community the origin of the trouble could invariably be traced back to 'an import' or 'blow in'.

The Roman Catholic school stood beside the local chapel on the outskirts of the village. Here the conditions were similar to ours. The pupils were taught by two teachers and the numbers attending were about the same. The only major difference was that their master was quite a quiet man and seldom used the cane. The assistant teacher, on the other hand, was a different kettle of fish. She was quite cross and was known throughout the area as the 'waterhen'. How she succeeded in attaining this illustrious nickname I don't know.

Looking through old school photographs of both village schools taken over fifty years ago, I find that fifty five per cent of the pupils left the area, sixteen per cent are dead, and the remainder are, gladly, still with us. Those who still survive include one doctor, one veterinary surgeon, two missionaries, six school teachers and three nurses. Strangely, there are no clergymen, priests or nuns, which doesn't say much for the reams of scripture and catechism we learned, not to mention the Latin roots.

Indeed, these studies did not end with day school. We all had our Catechisms – Roman Catholic, Methodist and Church of Ireland. I had to learn two, Church of Ireland and Methodist and I'm ashamed to admit that I don't remember any of it. Our church was three miles away so my sister and I attended the Methodist Sunday School on Sunday mornings and a Church of Ireland one for service in the Orange Hall on Sunday evenings followed by evening service. How I envied the Roman Catholic children who went to mass once on Sunday and that was it.

The little Methodist church was situated behind the village overlooking the fairgreen and only a matter of yards from my home. The procedure here was much the same every Sunday. First we gathered around the little organ and sang one or two children's hymns followed by prayer. We then divided into four classes with about five children in each and after Catechism we listened to Bible stories. Bible stories are enjoyed by children all over the world and many remain in our minds for the rest of our lives. The story of the birth of Christ will always be the favourite for children but others that remained in my memory were all associated with disasters in some form or other. The crucifixion of Christ, Daniel in the lions' den, the great flood, the plague of boils and the plague of frogs were all troublesome incidents that remained in my mind and probably caused a young boy a certain amount of distress for whenever we had continuous heavy rain and the Sillees river flooded, covering acres of land all around the village, it did cross my mind that it was about time someone should begin building an ark. I clearly remember coming out from Sunday school after hearing the story of the plagues expecting to see millions of frogs hopping around the fairgreen or to see many people in the village covered with boils. The children of the Sunday School sang at all the church functions and I well remember, at the age of seven, singing my first solo from the pulpit of this little church and I have received much pleasure from singing ever since.

On Sunday afternoons we made our way at four o'clock to Sunday School in the Orange Hall where the local Rector taught us. This was a boring affair, for 'Old Stothers', as he was affectionately known, was a Latin and Greek scholar and I never heard him relate a Bible story. We just read a verse of Scripture in turn for half an hour while he kept looking at his 'half-hunter' watch every few minutes; to relieve the monotony, we counted the number of times.

What would we do in Ireland without religion? It seems to play such an important part in our lives. It certainly absorbed many hours for the boys and girls of all denominations when we were growing up.

We liked to see visitors arrive at the school as they kept the Master in conversation. The School Attendance Officer, Barney 'Boxty' or the local Rector seemed to have a lot of time on their hands and would chat for maybe an hour. The school inspector, on the other hand, was not a welcome visitor. He asked questions on our work and if pupils did not answer correctly they were in dire trouble afterwards, for poor answering would affect the Master's personal report.

Some pupils walked up to four miles to school in all weathers. Often their clothes and footwear were wet and there were no drying facilities. There was no electricity, nor even paraffin lamps. In the short dark days of winter we often worked in semi-darkness.

I never liked school, in fact I loathed it and the same could be said for all the other pupils, especially those under the jurisdiction of our Master; we were all terrified of him and he made life hell for many. Long after some of the boys and girls left school they would almost jump over the road hedge sooner than meet him. It was a great pity he couldn't control his temper and display more kindness and patience because he was a good teacher who could have been a better one.

Children playing on a fair day, while Sgt P. J. Farrell inspects the town, 1930s. (Ada Cassidy)

4   Village Pastimes

LEISURE CENTRES, community centres and sports centres did not exist during the 1930s. All weather pitches and children's playgrounds were unheard of. Track suits and exercise bicycles had yet to reach Derrygonnelly. We children amused ourselves and had our own pastimes and games. One thing was certain; we were never bored. Weather permitting we were never indoors and the day was never long enough. What did we do? What games did we play? We didn't play cowboys and Indians simply because we had never heard of them, as none of us had ever been to a cinema and comics didn't reach the village until 1937.

We found it difficult to play football since all the land around the village was owned by one farmer and if we entered any of his fields with a football we were promptly ejected and the ball confiscated. If we played football or handball on the village street or in the vicinity, the local police objected, although only one car a day might pass through. The fine at the local Petty Sessions for causing an obstruction by playing handball was two shillings and costs. We were allowed, however, to play marbles on the side-paths.

Horses were the principal mode of transport; there were no tractors and few cars, lorries or bicycles; so it was only natural when children imitated their elders that horses should be involved. We tied each other up with reins and ropes and pretended we were driving cart horses, race horses, quiet ones, wild ones, and horses working double and single. Sometimes you were the horse and sometimes the driver. We walked, trotted, galloped and pulled little carts for miles and we certainly did not require a lullaby when we finally went to bed. This was a time when most supplies came to the village by horse and cart from the railway station at Enniskillen, ten miles away. Every morning the village street was congested with horse-drawn vehicles hauling the farmers' milk to the local creamery or drawing turf from the bogs situated in the mountainous regions west of the village, so little wonder we imitated horses so much.

Gradually lorries replaced the horse and cart and hauled goods to the village, so it was natural that we began to imitate the lorry. Little four-wheeled vehicles appeared, one boy pushing while the other sat on it and steered, both making hideous noises which were supposed to imitate a lorry engine. One of the older boys, whose father was a carpenter, made a fairly large model of one of these contraptions. He managed to get a pair of old motorcycle wheels, minus the tyres, and two old bicycle wheels, also without tyres. Two tea chests mounted on a frame with the motorcycle wheels on the rear, together with the bicycle wheels on front and the usual rope steering, resulted in a spectacular but very unwieldy vehicle indeed. There were no brakes and no means of escape if this lethal means of transportation got away. Nevertheless, it was much in demand, so much so that my friend Hugh, who lived next door, was absolutely spellbound and managed to borrow it for a few days and parked it in his back yard. He managed to persuade me to push while he stood in the front tea chest steering and at the same time making grotesque noises imitating a lorry engine. Hugh was in his element while I had my head down at the rear, pushing with all my might and sweating profusely.

Our next door neighbour on the other side was the parish priest. As it happened, this gentleman was quite deaf as a result of his service as a padre in the First World War, where the continuous bombardment badly affected his hearing. The Sunday collection in those days was usually a penny each and the collections from all three chapels in the parish amounted to a very large number of pennies. The parish priest was wont to put all these pennies into one collecting box, which was a square, shallow, wooden container with a handle. He carried this box to the Bank which came to the village once a week for two hours.

On this particular morning Hugh climbed into his infernal

machine in the backyard and grabbed his steering rope, while I stationed myself at the rear ready to push. We charged out through the gravel-strewn archway making an awful racket with Hugh making his usual engine noise. I had my head down, pushing like mad, not knowing that the parish priest was on his way to the bank with his collecting box which contained about a thousand pennies. All I remember is that when we reached the footpath there was a crash and the contraption toppled over. When I looked up all hell began to break loose as I saw the parish priest spread-eagled over Hugh in the tea chest and a shower of pennies flying over the village street – pennies from heaven indeed! I took to my heels down the backyard and jumped the wall, where I stood on the bank of the river, shaking like a leaf and was soon joined by Hugh who was as white as a sheet. There we stood, too shocked to speak, waiting for the priest, my father and the local police sergeant to arrive with handcuffs. We must have stood in the mud for at least an hour wondering if we should throw ourselves in and end it all. Eventually we hauled ourselves out and decided to face the music, but strangely my father said nothing and neither did the sergeant, simply because nobody told them. Everyone in the village knew of the incident except my father, for no-one ever told him and the parish priest, bless his heart, never spilled the beans, although we spilled his pennies.

Hoop hurling was another favourite pastime. The spokes were taken out of a discarded bicycle wheel and with a short stick we propelled it along the footpath or up and down the street during the afternoons when traffic was almost non-existent. Some boys could guide a hoop around corners with great speed and dexterity whilst others managed to procure an old car tyre and this was considered a marked improvement on a bicycle wheel.

The local hardware merchant purchased a huge six ton AEC lorry which ran on what was know then as crude oil. A man from Enniskillen was engaged to drive this monster since the job was quite beyond the ability of any local. After some time one of the tyres became defective and was discarded. My friend Hugh was first on the scene and soon he was hurling this huge tyre around the village. Every time it fell it took at

least two boys to lift it. At the lower end of the village the street
has a gradual slope and at the bottom stood a large shed with
slatted sides used for drying timber from the mill. The proprietor of the mill, Old Willie, was building a boat in this shed and
one day, unknown to him, Hugh was hurling his monster tyre
down the street accompanied by several of us hurling hoops.
As usual he was making lorry engine sounds and perspiring
profusely with the effort. Then disaster struck, as the tyre
increased speed on the slope, went out of control, gathering
pace all the time, whilst leaving Hugh standing in bewilderment as it made its way straight for Willie's shed. There stood
Willie leaning over his beloved boat with his glasses on the end
of his nose, fixing another board to its side. Suddenly there
was a crash as Hugh's tyre tore a hole in the flimsy slats,
brushed against Willie's backside and crashed out the other
side coming to rest in the river. 'I thought it was the devil
himself', remarked Willie. The giant tyre remained in the river
until the flood took it away – maybe it ended up in the Atlantic
Ocean: another victim for St Faber!

St Faber's curse on our river did not deter us from fishing.
There were several places on the river near the village where
the odd roach, perch, pike or eel might be hooked. These
places were to be found at bends on the river known locally as
holes. There was the Brick (pronounced 'breek') Hole and
Mary Egg's Hole. But there must be something to St Faber's
curse for it was rare for a fish to be caught; the news travelled
quickly and we all cast our lines at that spot hoping that
perhaps we might be lucky too.

There was a fall in the river as it passed through the village
and the bed was made up of gravel, stones and silt. As small
boys we liked to catch striddlies and in this stretch of the river
they were plentiful. These little fish are better known as
minnows or sticklebacks but to us they were known for
generations as striddlies and they offered better sport than
bigger fish, for there were more of them. Here we could paddle
around in our bare feet lifting the flat stones to reveal these
little bearded creatures. Some boys, who were slick of hand,
could flick a small trout on to the bank.

Every household in the village owned at least one dog,
usually a terrier. They were of no particular breed of terrier,

just a mixture, yet were nevertheless specially bred for their ability to catch and kill rats since every household kept some kind of livestock in their backyard, cattle, horses, pigs or hens. The feeding of these animals, together with the close proximity of the river, resulted in a serious rat problem. These marvellous little dogs were quite wicked, but most affectionate and faithful towards their owners. They were seldom allowed into the home. They were fed once a day with anything left over at dinner time. Dog collars and leads were unknown; on one of my early visits to Enniskillen I remember a lady with a small dog on a lead and I thought it was the silliest thing I had ever seen and I had great sympathy for the little creature.

On Saturdays we occasionally set off over the hills to hunt rabbits and brought with us four or five of these little terriers to assist in this pursuit. Rabbits were plentiful but we made so much noise on our approach that they had ample time to be safely underground before we arrived. However, the terriers took up the scent, barking and whining while they clawed frantically at the rabbit burrow. We travelled for miles, covered with mud and scratches, enjoying the thrill of the chase. I don't ever remember catching a rabbit but we thoroughly enjoyed ourselves and returned home happy, hungry and tired.

Sometimes, probably through boredom, a disagreement arose between two or more dogs and a fight then developed. Within seconds all the others came scurrying out of entries, alleyways and laneways and soon they all joined in showing their teeth, their hair standing on end. There could be up to fifteen dogs biting and snapping at legs, ears and throats, some charging in, leaving their mark and then retreating again. The owners of the dogs never interfered. They just let them fight it out until eventually the dogs limped home to lick their wounds. If a strange dog was foolish enough to enter the village, the local terriers would gang up on him and if he didn't beat a hasty retreat pretty quickly he could be maimed for life. It must be years since I saw a vicious dogfight. Modern dogs, usually pure bred and fed on sophisticated dog foods, are so lethargic and lazy that they can scarcely walk. When they are not sleeping they are leaving huge piles on the footpaths.

My dog, a small black mongrel terrier, was named Toby. I was devoted to this little dog as indeed he was to me. Everywhere I went he trotted at my heels and came up the road to meet me as I came home from school. My father had land which was leased, about three miles from the village, from a spinster lady named Miss Trotter who lived alone. Every time I visited this farm with my father and Toby in attendance, to inspect the cattle, Miss Trotter made a great fuss of my dog and it was obvious that she had designs on him. Eventually she asked me if she could have him and I refused point blank. How did she expect any boy to part with his dog? My father, however, pointed out to me that she was an old lady who lived in a remote area and the dog would be good company for her, besides which I could get another one. It wasn't the done thing in those days to argue with one's parents, so I turned away with tears in my eyes and went home – dogless.

I didn't sleep a wink that night wondering how Toby was making out and swearing vengeance on Miss Trotter for coveting my dog, the only real thing I cherished and possessed. Without success, I tried not to cry because I had never heard of anyone crying over a dog although I did not realize, as my father did, that the old lady was desperately lonely and Toby would be her only companion. He would certainly be well looked after, even pampered. But didn't she realise that she had broken one of the commandments 'Thou shalt not covet thy neighbour's dog'? In the cold light of day I decided to take positive action. Instead of my father getting me another dog, I decided to get one myself so as to give it to Miss Trotter and secure the return of my beloved Toby.

Next day, when I went to school I made exhaustive enquiries of my schoolmates to see if they knew of anyone in the locality who had pups for giving away, but without success. Money never changed hands, in those days, for dogs or pups. Next day, however, a girl informed me that a gentleman, who lived at Blaney Mill near the shore of Lough Erne, had a litter of black and white terrier pups. I was overjoyed. I borrowed a large basket from my aunt which she used for bringing eggs to the shop. Early the following Saturday I set out to walk to Blaney. Luckily there were three pups left when I arrived and I was asked to choose one. I didn't much mind which one I took since it was not for myself but for my public enemy Number One, Miss Trotter, God rest her soul! Finally I selected a white one with a brown spot over his right ear which I loaded into my basket and set off for Miss Trotter's residence. She was surprised to see me and was still loath to part with Toby until she looked into the basket, 'I'll call him Spot', she said and I took off quickly without a backward glance, down the avenue with Toby at my heels. I arrived home hungry, tired and happy with a blister on my heel, having walked, in all, about ten miles, but every step was worth it. Toby was overjoyed to be reunited with his young master and familiar surroundings. Miss Trotter and Spot were faithful companions for many years and Toby lived to a ripe old age. Solomon in all his wisdom could not have come to a more amicable solution.

Like the boys with their horses and lorries, the young girls of the village also passed their spare time by imitating their elders. They played 'wee house', 'hospital', or 'shop'. The wee house was usually a corner of an outhouse or a small disused piggery. Cracked cups, old tea pots, curtains, old pots and pans and an assortment of discarded utensils were collected from around the village. The cupboards were old egg boxes and orange boxes. A makeshift fireplace and some stools completed the little kitchen. Imagination then ran riot as they talked of the parlour and who was coming to visit; they talked of the upstairs bedrooms and even the spare room and maid's room. They changed their names to more exotic ones. They talked of what they were going to have for dinner, probably several courses, and their imaginary husbands or boyfriends were all rich and famous with sissy names.

When playing hospital they made makeshift beds out of old wooden boxes which were laid side by side and covered with sacks and flour packs. Some of the girls were nurses who wore white aprons and tea cloths on their heads while others were patients stretched out on the beds, some moaning with pains in various parts of their anatomy. I remember one particular girl who seemed to know more about the facts of life than the rest of us and always insisted on being a patient. Her usual complaint was 'I have a pain in my head. I think I am going to have a baby'. This statement baffled us as we were sure that babies were found under cabbage heads, in fact we often searched the cabbage patch for ages to see if we could find one. Anyway, what had a pain in the head to do with it?

When playing shop the girls confined themselves to the drapery business which today they would call the fashion trade. They collected old dresses, hats and shoes from their parents. As the word got round, other girls from the village arrived for a fit-on and a fashion parade took place with the customers putting on snobbish accents. Of course they weren't allowed to take the merchandise away since it was kept for another day.

Street games such as hopscotch and queenio were played by the girls while boys played marbles on the footpath with earthenware marbles. Tig, rounders, robbers comin' thro' and others that I have forgotten were played by both boys and girls. As we had never been to a cinema not only were cowboys and Indians unknown to us but the glories of the Seventh Cavalry also escaped us until much later in life. Occasionally we played soldiers, especially after listening to poems and stories at school such as *The Charge of the Light Brigade, The Siege of Lucknow* or *The Burial of Sir John Moore.*

In those days all the boys wore short trousers and, when the seat wore thin, a large patch the size of a football was stitched on and this gave them a new lease of life. We all wore boots, some quite heavy with studs on the soles. On Sundays we wore light boots and maybe the odd sissy boy wore shoes. We wore stockings up to our knees to school except in very cold weather when we wore stockings over our knees and under the legs of our trousers rather like tights.

I once owned a pet rabbit which I named Jerry. Old Willie, one of the yard men, made a hutch for him and the children came to feed him with pieces of carrots and lettuce. He was the only pet rabbit in the village and was a great favourite. Sometimes I gave Jerry the run of our house where he enjoyed running up and down the stairs and through the rooms. Unfortunately someone left the back door open and my dog Toby came in. Jerry's lifeless body was found later on the landing. It is difficult to describe my feelings. I had just two pets and one had killed the other. However, I couldn't bring myself to beat the dog and we were all grief-stricken about Jerry as the news spread through the village and the children arrived to view his remains. The least we could do was to give him a decent funeral. Arrangements were made to hold the ceremony the following Saturday morning when, praise be, we had no school.

A large cardboard boot box was procured which was just the right size to hold Jerry. After it was suitably lined with cloth and decorated with ribbons the rabbit was placed inside and 'lay in state' until funeral time. A grave was dug at the bottom of the garden and at the appointed time four girls carried the makeshift coffin towards the garden. There Jerry was lowered into the grave while we all sang 'There is a happy land'. After Old Willie filled in the grave we erected a tombstone made from a tea chest lid with the deceased's name, age and date of death suitably inscribed on it.

My friend Hugh like most small children, had trouble with his first teeth when they began to decay and cause toothache. His mother therefore wisely decided to take him to a dentist in Enniskillen and have the offending teeth extracted. In 1934 this was considered a daunting experience for a small boy and so I was invited to accompany Hugh and his mother although it is doubtful if my presence gave him any comfort or reassurance. We duly arrived at the dentist's premises and were shown into the waiting room. While we were waiting patiently for the feared moment to arrive, Hugh announced that he wanted to go to the toilet, so we were directed to a little house in the backyard. Neither of us had ever seen a toilet like this before. This was not a hole in a wooden seat with a large bucket underneath. No! It was made of delph with a chain. Was this for pulling yourself up when you finished? Hugh sat down on the toilet seat and I caught the chain exclaiming 'that's a handy gadget for hauling yourself up' and gave it a sharp yank. Immediately a roaring rush of water appeared under the toilet seat and in sheer terror we both ran up the yard where we met a workman. I exclaimed to him breath-lessly 'That place is going to be flooded'. 'Don't worry sonny', he replied, 'It will stop itself'. This was our first experience of a flush toilet.

If there was a wedding in the local chapel and we weren't at school, we went with almost the entire population of the village to watch the proceedings. There were no morning suits or wedding gowns in those days. Nevertheless, the event impressed us so much that we had a 'pretend wedding' in some backyard that evening. There was competition for who would be bride and who would be groom although often one was not acceptable to the other. In addition there was often trouble as to who would officiate. Flowers were pinched from a local garden and the happy pair were driven away on a meal barrow.

Sex education was non-existent in our school or homes, yet, living in the country we couldn't help but see cattle, sheep horses, asses, goats and various pets mating and the resulting pregnancy and reproduction. This knowledge, together with information from older boys and girls, meant that we were much more advanced in this field than town or city children and we soon gave up searching for babies under cabbage heads.

At a very early age I witnessed and in some cases assisted in, the birth of calves, piglets, lambs, foals, kittens and pups. I did, however, often wonder how a chicken got into an egg.

Upper Main Street, Derrygonnelly in the 1930s.

5 Wandering Around

THERE ARE TIMES when a boy likes to wander about on his own, to just come and go as he pleases, walk around with his hands in his pockets, sometimes in a dream, stopping here and there to look around or ask a question. There were many places of interest in and around our small village and many interesting people to talk to, most of them willing to take time to talk to a small boy.

In the middle of the nineteenth century the local landlord erected a scutch mill operated by water power at the lower end of the village. When flax ceased to be grown the mill was converted into a saw mill and in my youth it was operated by a gentleman known throughout the district as Old Willie. Willie was a most intelligent man with great ingenuity. He had an inventive mind and looking back I can now see that he was ahead of his time in his ideas.

A visit to the saw mill was a fascinating experience. The Sillees River was diverted into the mill race by lowering great sluice gates and the water collected in a large dam. While the dam was filling up, the great driving belts were put on the pulleys of whatever saw was required. The largest was a four foot rip saw mounted on a great roller bench known as a rack bench. The large tree trunk was levered on to the bench and secured with wooden spuds in the proper position for a through and through cut.

At the lower end of the dam, and just outside the wall of the mill, stood the great water wheel with its axle and pinion reaching inside the building. When the dam was full, the belts on and the tree trunk in position, Willie opened the sluice gate and the water wheel began to turn, first slowly and then gathering speed with a deafening rumbling noise. No smoke,

33

steam, smell of oil or fumes, just pure clean water straight from the mountain lakes, propelling the mighty wheel.

Then Willie and his assistant Paddy slowly pushed the rack bench until the saw bit into the large tree trunk. The power of the water wheel was tremendous, for in a short time the tree was reduced to planks. The sluice gate was then closed again while the dam was replenished with water, belts were changed to the eighteen inch saw and guides set up to the proper measurement. When the water wheel was again started up, Willie and Paddy soon reduced the planks to four by two's or whatever measurement was required.

Local farmers who wanted to build a dwelling house or farm building simply cut down one or more suitable trees and hauled them to the mill where they were sawn into the required sizes. Most of the timber was soft wood such as larch, spruce or scotch fir although local hardwoods such as oak, elm and ash were also used. Sometimes more intricate work was required, such as cutting out felloes from ash for cart wheels and then the band saw was used. Trindles or solid wooden wheels for turf barrows or bow rails for carts were also cut on the band saw from both ash and larch. Other intricate work required the belts to be hitched up to the pulleys of the lathe when large pieces of elm were reduced to make naves to house the axles on cart wheels.

As small boys we often required a pair of wooden wheels for a little barrow or cart; so we approached old Willie and if he was in a good mood he cut them out on the band saw. Our timing had to be just right. We judged his mood, when he had just finished using the band saw and if water was plentiful.

In the early days of the wireless, wet batteries were required to run the sets. A wet battery lasted about a week depending on how often the wireless was used, so Willie built a small water wheel which rotated quite fast on a small amount of water which continually flowed underneath the mill. This wheel in turn drove a small dynamo which charged the batteries for those wealthy people who could afford a wireless.

When I had seen all I wanted to see at the mill I strolled just around the corner to Pat's workshop which was originally the old mill school. Pat was a man of many talents. He was a carpenter, a wheelwright and a stonemason. The first thing that struck you on entering his workplace was the beautiful smell of timber and red lead paint. The workshop was spacious with benches which were littered with various tools of the trade up each side. A stack of timber lay against the gable wall and a partly finished horse cart stood in the centre, whilst completed cart wheels, windows, turf barrows and maybe a child's cradle were neatly stacked at the other gable.

Not everybody was welcome in the workshop. There were those who just couldn't keep their hands to themselves. They lifted sharp tools thus ruining the edge and moreover risked causing danger to themselves. These boys were well known throughout the village and were not welcome in any workplace. Your only chance of being accepted was to go alone and keep your hands in your pockets and your mouth shut. Ask a few questions by all means but they had to be sensible ones.

Horse carts were always in demand as those were the days before the tractor. Most people could tell who built a particular cart by its shape and design. The ideal cart was one that was strong, light and well balanced. The balance, in other words, the positioning of the wheels and axle, was most important. If this position was not 'spot on' then the cart was either too light or too heavy at the back. Some small farmers, especially those with wet land, kept a lighter type of horse and therefore required what was known as 'a handy cart'.

Most times when I wandered into Pat's workshop there was a cart in the process of being built. He seemed to tolerate my questions, 'Who was he building the cart for?', 'What kind of timber was that?' and so on. Different tradesmen used different timbers; Pat used larch or deal for the shafts and sheeting. Sometimes if the cart was used for hauling stones or gravel it was sheeted with poplar or sally which had more 'give' in it.

The most interesting part of the whole process was the building of the wheels. The wheel consisted of six curved felloes, made from ash, and when dowelled together they formed the rim. There were twelve spokes made from oak and the nave or centre was made from elm. Each end of the spoke was rectangular while the remainder was oval and fashioned with a spoke shave. Mortices were gouged out of the felloes and nave to fit the spokes but they were fitted in such a way that the whole wheel dished outwards. Pat had a small axe or hatchet with an edge like a lance which he used with great dexterity to round off sharp edges, for every wheelwright had his own style.

During summer when the weather was good, Pat was out around the countryside building and doing repairs. He spent the winter in his workshop. Pat's youngest son Jack was a few years older than my pals and me. He was a useful boy to know for he often made or repaired little carts and barrows for us in his father's workshop.

When we left Pat's premises and walked a few yards up the village street we came to the humble establishment of McFadden the tailor. He was never addressed as 'Mr' McFadden and no-one seemed to know what his first name was or even where he came from, since he wasn't local. He was a small delicate little man. Some looked on him with a certain amount of suspicion, I suppose because he was an 'import' and others described him as 'a harmless wee man'. McFadden didn't object to a boy wandering around his little workshop as long as you didn't stand between him and the window thus blocking the light. He greeted you with a smile as he sat cross-legged on a low bench hand-sewing a suit of clothes. In a corner stood a tailor's dummy partially dressed in thick melton or tweed. Several large smoothing irons and an ancient sewing machine comprised his entire tools of the trade. The bench against the wall was littered with reels of thread, boxes of buttons, padding, lining and suit lengths waiting to be made up. Wee McFadden was always busy because he 'worked cheap' and had a sizeable family to support. There were few ready-made suits in the early 1930s so the tailor was in good demand. The clients were more concerned with how long it lasted than with style. A Sunday suit might change colour several times with age.

Across the street from McFadden was another tailor. Jack operated from an upstairs room over his brother's grocery shop so there was no chance of a visit there. Jack was both deaf and dumb and led a lonely life, but in the mornings when his brother and sister were at early mass he played children's games with the boys and girls before we went to school. Often on wet mornings while we sheltered in an archway, Jack tried to teach us the deaf and dumb alphabet. I expect he longed to communicate with us, for in those days many people who were handicapped were ignored and Jack worked alone all day in his upstairs workroom.

My favourite haunt for a visit was Sammy's establishment which was part shop and part workshop. He was the local saddler and harness maker and he also sold boots and fishing tackle. Heavy nailed boots for farmers and farm workers were always in demand, so were the lighter sparable boots (less heavily nailed) and the still lighter ones for Sunday wear. He also sold boots for boys and leather of various qualities.

The fishing tackle consisted of just three sizes of hook; small ones for making flies suitable for trout fishing; eel hooks for perch, roach and eels; and large ones for pike. He also stocked fishing lines of various strengths, reels and lengths of gut. Few locals fished for trout and if we went to Carrick Lake or Lough Erne for a day's fishing, especially when the perch were schooling, we just brought a hook and line, not forgetting a cork out of a Guinness bottle and a tin of worms. When we arrived at the lake shore we simply cut a long hazel rod out of a hedge or thicket and we were ready to fish. No stools, fishing baskets or large umbrellas were needed and we would run a mile from those hideous maggots.

The far end of the shop was the harness workshop. This consisted of a work bench, a fairly high stool with an old cushion on it and the various tools strewn over the bench or hanging on the wall. An essential piece of equipment to the saddler was a wooden contraption which he held between his knees and closed like a vice in order to hold the piece of leather he was working on. This piece of equipment was known as a 'clam'.

A little stove glowed red in the corner and made the place very cosy and it was a grand place to go on a cold, wet day. How I envied Sammy working here all day while I had to go to school! The floor was littered with harness; some newly made, some to be repaired and some waiting to be collected by the owners. Sheets of harness leather of various qualities and thickness lay against the wall. The smell of leather was the first thing that hit your nostrils as you entered Sammy's domain and then Sammy's smile as he looked at you over his wire-rimmed glasses.

I was always made welcome in his cosy place of work for he often sought my help for various jobs. 'Just the man I'm looking for' was his usual welcome. I was proud to be called a man at eight years old and was also pleased that he sought my help for various tasks, one of which was waxing the hemp. A large roll of hemp was produced and a number of strands about one metre long were twisted together into one. I held one end and Sammy held the other while he rubbed wax up and down the length of the hemp until it was completely waxed from one end to the other. The number of strands varied according to its use; most cart harness took seven strands and a light bridle about four. The finished waxed hemp was now completely waterproof and each end was attached to special needles. Sammy was ready to begin. He climbed up on his high stool, put the clam between his knees and inserted the section of harness to be repaired. He bored holes with his awl and inserted the needles from each side, pulling the hemp through. This was known as double stitching. It was extremely strong and would last for years.

Another job I got was teasing horse hair which was used for stuffing horse collars, straddles and saddles. Where did the supply of horse hair come from? Many farmers who owned a large acreage of rough land reared and broke in young horses. These wild young animals were brought in for breaking in when they were around two and a half years old and their manes and tails were long and thick. The surplus hair was pulled out so that they had a nice switch tail and a tidy mane. This surplus hair was sold to the saddler. The hair grew again and a tidying up operation took place every year. Whenever a horse died farmers often cut off the tail and mane hair and tried to palm it off on the saddler but this dead hair, as it was called, was useless to the saddlery trade. Sometimes they tried mixing it with 'live' hair. Farm workers often regarded the sale of horse hair as a perk. So when I got the job of teasing I was warned by Sammy to look out for the inferior stuff, especially if it came from a doubtful source.

The most important part of a set of harness was the collar. If the collar was in bad repair or not fitting properly, it damaged the horse's shoulder sometimes down to the raw flesh. A horse was required, during summer, to mow from four o'clock in the morning, and then haul the milk to the creamery. It was hitched to the haymaking machinery for the rest of the day. This could be repeated day after day in good weather so if the harness didn't fit properly severe damage to the horse's flesh occurred and the farmer was in trouble. Most of the farmers in our area owned small farms and just kept one horse. If the animal met with misfortune and couldn't work this was a major disaster, so it was essential that the animal was well looked after and that the harness fitted properly. The straddle supported the full weight of the load on the horse's back so its quality was also important and the same applied to the breeching as it kept the cart back when going down hill. If this piece of equipment broke then the cart ran up against the horse's hindquarters and a serious accident could occur, especially if carrying a heavy load.

Some farmers were noted for their carelessness, their harness was tied together with string and wire and the cart axle screeched for want of grease.

So Sammy's craftmanship was most important to the farming community and his reputation was always on the line. Most of his work was repairs to cart and driving harness, but I was more intrigued by watching him make a new set and dropped in each day to see the different parts take shape. Sometimes I just sat in front of the little red hot stove on a winter's day and watched a pair of traces take shape under Sammy's skilful hands or saw him finish off a new set with brass or silver coloured mountings for decoration.

A Fermanagh blacksmith at work (Ulster Folk and Transport Museum/Fermanagh County Museum).

6   *The Forge*

FOR A CHANGE of scenery and faces, especially on a cold day, the forge was another of my favourite haunts. The building was long and low, with corrugated iron walls and an asbestos roof. It was the last of many forges in the neighbourhood, over many generations, and was situated at the rear of the village in a place known as the Commons. When you entered the forge you were met with the glow and heat of the fire, the smell of horse and human sweat, the smell of red hot iron when dipped in water, and the smell of burning horse hooves and horse dung.

This establishment was run by two brothers, Eddie and Charlie, assisted by their nephew, Andy. Andy was known by his surname Flaherty. Eddie was a powerfully built man with a broad chest and thick strong arms and he was the boss. The forge had a fire and bellows at each end and both were used when they were busy. The fire was situated on a platform built of stone; a large bellows was operated by levering a long handle up and down and was attached to the fire by a wide pipe or passage. A large stone trough was built into the platform which was filled with water.

I wasn't allowed to stand around too long before I was given the job of operating the bellows. This wasn't just a matter of levering the handle up and down any old way. If you did it too frequently, then too much coal was used to no useful purpose; if you levered too slowly, then not enough heat was generated to make the iron red hot. Special smiths' coal was used, yet to me it looked as if it was just ordinary slack but I'm sure there was something special about it.

There were always a few of the village's old age pensioners standing around the fire discussing the country's problems while Johnnie, an old soldier, related his exploits in the Boer War when he served with the old 27th.

Most farmers chose a wet day, when work on the farm was slack, to bring their horses to be shod. This annoyed Charlie and Eddie as they had to handle the horse's wet hairy legs while the water dripped off the horse's body onto the back of their shirts. Very often they just let the horse stand there until he 'drip-dried', much to the annoyance of the farmer. They preferred a dry day when the shoeing could be done outside where there was more room to manoeuvre and where it was much cooler.

When things were slack they made the shoes of various sizes and hung them on the wall in groups of four. Large shoes for the big hairy-legged Clyde, smaller for the Irish draught type, smaller still for cobs and ponies and, not forgetting, shoes for asses, for there were many of these noble animals in the area. The local hardware merchant supplied the blacksmith with various thicknesses of horse shoe iron, different sizes of horse shoe nails, frost nails and cogs for use on slippery roads. He also supplied various widths of wheel-shoeing iron and, of course, smith's coal. Charlie took a long length of horse shoe iron and marked it off with chalk, in the required lengths for the new shoe. Then, while Flaherty held the cutter, Eddie gave it a mighty thump with a seven pound sledge hammer and this was repeated until the makings of many shoes lay on the floor. The four lengths were then put in the fire, the bellows put into operation and soon they were red hot. They were taken out with long-handled pincers, placed on the anvil where Charlie and Eddie, one with a heavy hammer and the other with a four pounder, struck the iron time about, while it gradually took on the proper form. The iron was heated several times before the horse shoe took its final shape. The last operation was punching the nail holes, four on one side and three on the other, heels and toe caps were hammered out and the shoe was hung on the wall ready for a customer. I can still hear the two distinct sounds of the light and heavy hammers on the anvil – in fact on a clear day this sound could be heard several miles away.

The blacksmiths knew most horses in the area; they knew if they were docile, nervous or just plain vicious. They didn't like to see a young horse appear, which had never been shod before. The owner was asked to lift each foot before they attempted to do so. When a farmer was breaking in a young horse, lifting each foot regularly was part of the process so that he would be quiet when brought to the forge. If a horse was difficult to shoe and some could be quite dangerous, then a twitch was inserted on their upper lip; the idea was that by twisting the twitch,the pain on his lip was so great that it kept its mind off the shoeing operation. One particular farmer had an ass with a blind eye. The blind eye was the least of the ass's faults for he was both vicious and evil and wouldn't let a blacksmith near him even on the blind side, twitch or no twitch. He lashed out with both front and hind legs and was also known to bite. It was a major operation to shoe this atrocious animal and when it arrived at the forge, the three blacksmiths cursed and swore time about while the news quickly spread around the village that this notorious animal was in the forge. They approached the animal as near as possible on the blind side and looped ropes on his legs; then a sharp pull and it fell to the floor with its good eye down. Its legs were secured, the owner lay on the ass's head and soon it had a new set of shoes.

The forge was a centre of subtle entertainment. If someone told you a story which you weren't inclined to believe, then you enquired 'Did you hear that in the forge?'. It was from the forge that most outlandish rumours and gossip originated. The method they used was special: two or three farmers, while waiting to have their horses shod exchanged news and gossip with each other and at the same time listened to the blacksmiths conversing with each other, in case they might pick up another snippet of news or gossip.

If Charlie, Eddie and Flaherty thought there was a gullible one amongst them they kept on working and at the same time carried on a conversation amongst themselves which consisted of lies, tall stories and false rumours, usually about the most unlikely local people. The farmer in turn told the stories around his own locality and soon they spread all around the area and further afield. It was surprising the number of people believed them but many knew that if they originated in the forge you just repeated them for a joke.

Eddie was a big man with lots of surplus flesh. He worked

clothed in shirt and trousers and canvas apron. When youths arrived at the forge, with maybe an ass or two to be shod, they stood beside their animals and said nothing for they were usually very shy, especially when they came from outside the village. Eddie would walk past the youth and put his hand under his fleshy arm pit gently squeezing his arm; this operation resulted in a noise resembling a fart; he repeated this action several times and then said to Charlie within the youth's hearing 'That young fella is full of farts, did ye hear him?' 'Indeed I did', Charlie repeated 'He should go to see the doctor', 'He could explode in his sleep' said Flaherty in a concerned voice. The farting continued until eventually the youth was almost reduced to tears of frustration in his innocence.

Shoeing a horse was an exacting trade – one slip and the animal could end up lame. The old set of shoes were prised off with a large pair of pincers after first loosening the clinched nails. The hoof was then cleaned and dressed by means of a hoof knife. A suitable set of shoes was selected and one by one they were heated red hot in the fire. The red hot shoe was pressed on the bare hoof until it burned a groove which enabled the shoe to fit snugly. It was then cooled in water and was ready for hammering on. It was important when driving in the shoe nails that they didn't hit the quick, otherwise the horse would be lame for weeks or, worse still, an infection could set in, but I never knew this to happen in our forge. After the nailing, the hoof received a final dressing from the rasp, a rub of old black oil with a paint brush and the job was completed.

Shoeing cart wheels was another essential job done by the blacksmith and Eddie waited until a number had accumulated before he embarked on this task and then an entire day was devoted to it. This was an outdoor task, so a cool, dry day was ideal.

Farmers who brought wheels to be shod were required to bring three bags of turf for each wheel. The operation took place a few yards from the forge beside a spring well. Here lay a large circular stone resembling a mill stone with a hole in the centre which was filled with water. The shoeing iron was cut, in the forge, the length of the circumference of the wheel. It was then bent into a circular shape and when both ends were reddened in the fire they were joined together by severe beating with the seven pound hammer. This was a tricky business for the resulting hoop had to be completely circular and the exact size of the wheel.

The hoop was then brought to the shoeing site outside and laid on the ground while turf was heaped around it and lit. After the turf fire around the rim was going for some time, it became red hot and ready to be placed on the wheel which lay on the circular stone. The rim was made to be an exact fit for the wheel taking into consideration the expansion when heated. In a process of burning and hammering it was fitted snugly onto the wheel and rotated quickly in a perpendicular position on the water in the centre hole in case too much of the wood burned. Not only was shoeing wheels precision work but it was also really tough physical work.

The blacksmiths worked six days a week, but in the evening and on Sundays each of them had their own hobbies and pastimes. Eddie was a coarse fisherman and every Sunday afternoon he and his friend, Pat, the carpenter, walked the two miles to Carrick Lake where they had a boat. They carried a tin of worms, a line, hooks and a cork each in their pocket. When they reached the shore they cut a hazel pole out of a thicket, for the lake was surrounded by hazel and alder. Often there was no need to cut one since there were usually many discarded along the shore. No fishing umbrellas, baskets, nets or stools; Eddie and Pat travelled light. They rowed their little boat to a selected area of the lake, lit their pipes, baited their hooks and fished. Conversation was limited as they simply enjoyed the peace, beauty and tranquillity of the area in their own way.

Eddie occasionally reared a greyhound and if he happened on a good one he raced it at Clones. He once owned a very famous greyhound called Golden Saddle which won many races and was sold for a tidy sum after which Eddie celebrated for a week.

Charlie and Flaherty on the other hand, were game fishermen. Charlie kept a little boat on Doagh Lake about four miles away and this small lake was noted for its brown trout. I watched Charlie many times sitting at his front room window tying flies. It was difficult to imagine the hands that wielded the heavy hammers in the forge so deftly tying the little feathers of different colours on the tiny trout hooks. He knew from the weather and the sky whether to go fishing or not, what lake to fish and even what part of it. He passed on his knowledge and could be seen regularly teaching the boys of the village to cast a line. They practiced their casting from one side of the street to the other and he would say 'Always cast your line so that the fly drops on the water like a snowflake.' As well as being an expert with the rod, he was also an expert with the gun. He knew every inch of the surrounding area, mountains or lowland, and when and where various game could be found.

He loved nature and studied the wildlife. He never read a book in his life and had little education, nevertheless he was so rich in knowledge. He knew the name of every bird, where they came from, and where they flew off to in winter. As children we often joined Charlie at the bridge when he pointed out the wildlife that abounded in the river and along its banks.

Like his brother Eddie, he was a dog lover. He kept a little spaniel that accompanied him to the forge every day and which slept on a bag of turf. He also owned a pointer and all the dogs in the household were well cared for, obedient and kept under strict control.

Charlie was an accomplished drummer and was leading drummer in St Patrick's flute band. His drum rolls were a joy to hear. Just before the 12th of July the members of the local Orange band brought their drums to Charlie to be repulled and tuned. On the 12th morning he was to be seen on the street listening critically to the drums and the drumming. It was difficult to imagine such nimble wrists on a man of such massive strength.

I lived for a number of years next door to the blacksmith's little two-up and two-down residence and at night, when I became bored with my homework, I wandered in for a bit of crack. By this time I was in my early teens and I suppose I might have been better occupied sticking to my homework; nevertheless, these visits were in a way an education in themselves.

The little kitchen was about twelve feet by twelve and had a hearth fire with a crane crook and a flagged floor. Here they sat, cooked, prepared and ate their meals. A small dresser stood against the back wall which together with a table, bench and a few chairs and stools were the entire furnishings. A paraffin lamp hung from a chain over the table. The little kitchen was usually packed with ceilidhers especially during the winter months when there was a row of seats around two walls and another row on stools in front of them. Eddie sat by the table with one of his cronies playing draughts, while Charlie regaled his visitors with hunting or fishing stories and maybe a ghost or fairy story now and again. They had another brother, Joe, who had just retired from the railways in Scotland. He had such a broad Glasgow accent that the natives didn't understand everything he said. He was both cook and housekeeper.

Pat was a nightly visitor and so were Sandy, Tommy and Tippie. Pat always sat in the same place at the back wall beside the dresser and contentedly smoked his pipe and like most pipe smokers of his day he spat regularly into the ashes beside the fire in the open hearth. There was of course a row of visitors sitting on stools between him and the hearth; however, this was no obstacle to Pat as he pursed his bottom lip and with a smart smack bobbed the spit over the heads of his friends in front, never once allowing one splash to hit them. This went on at regular intervals, each blob of spit alighting in the ashes in an area not much larger than a saucer. I tried many times to imitate this feat, but the spittle just ran down my chin. Some years later while serving in the Far East an instructor endeavoured to teach us the capabilities of mortars and artillery guns. It was explained that the shells travelled in a trajectory and should land in as concentrated an area as possible which was known as the 'beaten zone'. My mind immediately travelled back a few thousand miles and a few years to Pat and the spit pattern he made in the ashes; Pat's beaten zone!

The creamery, Derrygonnelly, c. 1910.

7 *More People and Places*

IF WE TRAVELLED up the village street another few yards we arrived at Dinnie Hugh's bicycle repair shop. Dinnie lived with his father and mother, two brothers and three sisters; quite a houseful of adults. Dinnie and Hugh were his Christian names. The small workshop was packed with bits and pieces of bicycles and a cluttered workbench piled high with heavy working boots awaiting half soles, heels, tips, toe plates and studs, for he was also a cobbler. It was a proud man who owned a good bicycle, for many of them were old wrecks and were made up from bits and pieces of many models. Dinnie Hugh spent most of his time patching up these crocks in order to keep them on the road. Fixing punctures also took up a lot of his time, since the roads were bad and the rubber in the tyres was of poor quality.

The local police ran a running battle with the cyclist – no bell; bad brakes; no front light or tail light at night; carrying a passenger on the bar or carrier; all meant that you climbed the steps to the Petty Sessions on the fourth Friday of the month. If you were caught, then the usual fine was two shillings with one shilling costs. So Dinnie Hugh did his best to keep these machines on the road. He was also kept busy patching up boots to keep people on the road, not to mention answering silly questions from inquisitive boys like me. He was an essential man in the community.

At the top of the village stood a small building known as the electric house. This was where the electricity supply to the village was generated by a gas engine which ran a dynamo giving direct current. The engine was run by special coal that produced gas and the pressure drove the pistons just like a steam engine. The engine was started up by Tom at dusk and stopped around midnight. There were many breakdowns and on a stormy night wires were sometimes blown down amidst a shower of sparks. Tom allowed us to stand at the door and look in but not to wander around as there were no safety guards on the fly-wheel or belts in those days. He never left the oil can out of his hand and squirted oil on everything that moved. The consumers only received current when the engine was operating. If Tom ever became ill or was the worse for drink, then there was no electricity for maybe a week, so we all reverted to lamps and candles. Just before the war the engine was changed to diesel and indirect current.

There were many servant boys and shop boys in and around the village during the 1930s and often they were at a loss for somewhere to go in the late evenings and nights. The electric house was one of their favourite haunts, as it was warm and dry and the crack was good. It was here the young men learned to play cards. Halfpenny brag was the favourite game. When a new shop assistant arrived in the the village to serve his time or a young farm worker came from the country, he eventually made his way to the electric house where he was initiated into the fraternity. He was required to stand in front of the furnace and at a given signal old Tom lifted the lid with the tongs. A belch of flame and gas shot to the ceiling and at the same time one of the boys would give the victim a terrific slap on the top of his head with an open hand. The young man, not familiar with these infernal machines, suffered from shock and frustration and wasn't at all clear what had happened to him!

Some houses in the village were not connected to the electricity since it proved expensive and unreliable and others had just one light in the kitchen, which at the best of times was scarcely bright enough to read by.

Across the road from the electric house stood the egg store which belonged to one of the leading merchants of the village. All the little grocery shops and travelling shops purchased eggs from the farmers but this establishment was the only one that shipped eggs to Belfast and Liverpool. Tommy and Phonso were the two men who worked in the egg store, sometimes helped by Sandy from the timber yard. Every egg was examined individually by placing it in front of a small circular aperture on a box-like contraption. Inside the box was a lighted candle so that Phonso could see if the egg was sound, rotten, cracked or even contained a chick. This operation was done at great speed by lifting four eggs at a time in each hand. They were then graded for size and finally packed in straw in large crates labelled ready for dispatch to the seven o'clock train from Enniskillen the next morning. In the early days they were transported to the railway station by horse and cart and later in the 1930s by lorry. With the coming of a more reliable electricity service the testing and grading became more efficient and the packing methods also improved.

The cracked eggs were sold very cheaply to the poorer people. This helped greatly to balance their budget as potatoes and eggs formed an important part of their diet.

Although the egg store was an interesting place for a young boy to spend a half hour on a wet day, Davie the boss did not tolerate visitors and sent us on our way pretty quickly. If the boss was away we might succeed in obtaining a few rotten eggs which we pelted at some unfortunate boys we didn't like. Sometimes we slipped one into a boy's pocket making sure that it broke by pushing him against a wall or such like. The stench of a rotten egg was horrific. The experience of sitting down to have a boiled egg for your tea and on chipping off the top to find it rotten inside, was not a pleasant one either and it happened quite frequently.

The next place of interest on the two hundred yards of village street was Davis's barber shop. Davis was his Christian name but he was better known by his nickname, the 'Hoozle'. He was an old soldier of the First World War, during which he was twice decorated for bravery with the Military Medal and Bar. When he was serving in France he had a dog which he named Hoozle and the dog followed him everywhere. Alas, the poor dog was killed in battle and Davis survived to be given the dog's name which stuck to him until he himself passed away.

As well as being a barber, Davis was a part-time postman, caretaker of the local graveyard, supervisor of the local water supply, and caretaker of the local Orange Hall. He also looked after a smallholding and if he had time to spare he repaired, bought and sold clocks and watches.

A young boy who wandered into Davis's little shop was immediately transported into another world. It was cluttered with all kinds of curios, pictures, clocks and all the paraphernalia of the barber's trade, together with the tools of the clock repairer. On the mantlepiece stood other nick-nacks, including a row of false teeth. Where did the false teeth come from? They came from the local graveyard, for when Davis was supervising the opening of a grave he collected these valuable relics which normally don't deteriorate very quickly, if at all. Indeed I once witnessed him trying to fit a set into an old chap's toothless mouth. It was only done as a joke but at the time I didn't recognise him with a mouthful of glittering teeth.

Davis was the drum major of the local Orange flute band and on the 12th of July his soldierly figure appeared in front of the band dressed in white flannel trousers, white pullover, orange sash, band cap, and his campaign medals glittering on his chest as he swung the mace vigorously.

The old graveyard, situated on the outskirts of the village, has been in use for over three hundred years and is now a good three feet higher than the surrounding field because of all the people buried there. When a member of the community passed away, a few of the neighbours turned up to dig the grave, under Davis's supervision. The word soon got around that a grave was being dug and the boys and girls made their way to the graveyard to see what the grave would reveal when opened. When the grave diggers got down to about four feet the skeleton of the last person interred appeared. Then one digger might exclaim 'there's oul John now' while the other might say 'not at all man, he's in the next grave, that's oul Maggie'. Underneath the top skeleton was a mass of bones from previous members of the family, and all the skulls, tibiae, femurs, ribs and shoulder blades were put in a neat pile on the side of the grave with no attempt made to hide or keep them from public view. Someone might remark 'Look at that for a set of teeth' as he kicked over a skull, 'He must have been reared on oaten bread', while Davis hovered around on the look out for another set of false teeth. For some of the young girls who intended to follow a career in the nursing profession the experience was indeed a helpful lesson in anatomy!

The following day the funeral took place, when every home

in the area was represented and again the genealogy of the family with relation to the skulls and bones might be discussed. All this might sound undignified and irreverent, but it was done in all innocence.

The creamery was a constant hive of industry and a visit was always a fascinating experience for a young boy. Most of the activity took place in the mornings while we were all at school but we could go during the holidays and on Saturdays.

The land which surrounds our village is inclined to be wet and not suitable for tillage but it does grow an abundance of grass and is excellent for milk production. Our creamery was therefore a very important establishment in the economy of the whole community.

Around half past ten in the morning the creamery was in full swing. A queue of carts, spring carts and wheelbarrows stretched right out to the road all waiting their turn to have their milk emptied, tested and weighed. Some farmers occasionally allowed one of us to drive the horse or ass a few yards at a time up the queue as far as the platform while a group of them exchanged the local news and gossip when awaiting their turn. After their cans had been emptied, the cart then moved around to the back of the creamery where the farmer received his quota of skim from Old Barney. Barney was a cranky old fellow. It was extremely difficult to manoeuvre an ass and cart as this noble animal was inclined to be stubborn, but if you stopped the cart in the wrong position you were 'for it'. The skim was brought home and used for the feeding of pigs and calves and baking bread.

The machinery was run by a steam engine and Willie the engineer watched over it with loving care, applying lubricating oil to all the moving parts and wiping the equipment with an old rag until it was spotless. By interchanging belts and pulleys the separator was run in the mornings and then in the afternoon the cream was put into the large churn, the belts changed and the churn rumbled around. After a couple of hours the butter was taken out and either wrapped in one pound packs or packed in fifty six pound boxes by the dairy maid.

The staff didn't object to a young boy wandering through the building, watching the thick cream streaming from the separator or the great churn rotating, but the manager, old

Beggs, was a very gruff man and quickly sent us on our way. So we just strolled around outside and a farmer might allow us to drive the ass and cart down the street. If this happened we felt really important.

Once the engineer asked the committee for more pay but they refused. In the early days engineers were scarce so when he went on strike the creamery came to a halt. This was a disastrous situation for the farmers, which is why another member of the staff volunteered to operate the engine. He shovelled lots of coal into the furnace and quickly got up steam while the carts queued up outside. Soon the pressure became so great that suddenly a great cloud of vapour belched out of the escape valve with a great hissing noise. The amateur engineer panicked and ran outside shouting at the top of his voice 'Run like hell, boys! The creamery is going to blow up'. Farmers ran in all directions trying to extricate their horses and asses, while milk cans spilled all over the place and carts knocked into each other. Needless to say, the engineer got his pay rise.

Ice cream came to the village around 1935 when a lady who kept a small confectionery and newspaper shop purchased a small wooden churn. The little churn rotated inside a container and the space between was packed with small chunks of ice which were replenished as they melted. The ice came by train from Belfast to Enniskillen and then to Derrygonnelly on the railway's lorry. It took a long time to churn the ice cream so we took it in turns to turn the handle and were rewarded with a free cone when the task was completed. The supply of ice was inclined to be irregular; so if there was no ice, there was no ice cream.

A few minutes' stroll past the creamery brought us to a neat house a few yards from the river bank with a green lawn and flowers in front and a vegetable garden to the rear. To the side of the house stood a small workshop and a visit here was an education. This was where Ernie carried on his many trades and his workshop was packed with all kinds of tools and gadgets. He attempted any task and was a superb story-teller. I could listen to his exaggerations for hours.

He cut hair; shaved; pulled teeth; mended footwear, schoolbags and harness; laid out corpses; bred ferrets and canaries, and fixed bicycles and musical instruments. He was also a keen gardener, a good cook and above all very intelligent.

If a farmer broke part of his harness on his way to the creamery or the bog, he called with Ernie who mended it while he waited. If you wanted a good close haircut or a loose tooth yanked out you received instant attention. Many of the men in the area just shaved once a week and therefore Ernie was quite busy every Saturday so that they looked well for Sunday. Shaving off their week-old stubble required a sharp edge on his cut throat razor and I winced as he caught the tip of their nose between his finger and thumb and bent it back in order to shave their upper lip.

If you wanted a patch on your wellingtons, a puncture mended on your bicycle or a pair of half-soles on your shoes, you received prompt service with a few good yarns.

I was fascinated by Ernie's canaries and visited his premises often to see how many eggs his breeding birds laid and how many hatched. In good weather he hung the cages, containing the good singing birds, outside and their song was a joy to hear. I also liked to watch the ferrets but didn't go too close, for some of the older boys told me that they might catch you by the throat and refuse to let go. One of Ernie's pastimes was roaming the rocky slopes of Carrick and Largalinny, with his ferrets, in search of rabbits.

Like all villages, we in Derrygonnelly had our characters. At the opposite end of the village stood a one-room, thatched cabin, the humble abode of another old soldier affectionately known as Frank Soup. Most people just addressed him as 'Soup'. Soup was a regular soldier before the First World War and at one time was a member of the Regimental Fife and Drum band. He was badly wounded at Gallipoli and thereafter walked with a limp. He supplemented his small disability pension by mending shoes and boots. He was far from being a craftsman and did a cheap, rough job. I loved visiting Soup, especially if he was cooking a meal on his little hearth. If it was a 'fry' he didn't bother putting the cooked food on a plate, he just ate it off the pan with his fingers; this saved washing up and the pan was never cleaned.

Sometimes he decided to cook a proper meal consisting of meat, potatoes and vegetables, and I watched the operation with amazement. He procured three empty, seven-pound,

corned beef tins and screwed them together and then to the
bunch of tins he attached a broom handle. In one tin he put the
meat, maybe a cheap end of bacon, in the other the vegetables,
usually swede or cabbage and in the third, potatoes. He then
lifted the lot by means of the broom handle and set them on the
fire to cook. They all cooked together giving off an appetising
aroma. As a small boy I really envied Soup and his way of life.

Soup was a valued member of St Patrick's Flute Band, but
because he lived alone in adverse conditions his turn-out was
not as clean and tidy as some of the other members demanded.
One summer Sunday the band decided to go to the nearby
seaside resort of Bundoran. On that particular morning, however, Soup discovered that he hadn't a clean shirt. This was the
age when men wore hard fronts and hard collars; so Soup got
out his old collar and front, whitewashed it and put it out in the
morning sunshine to dry.

Before embarking on the wagonette the band played
through the village and Soup looked resplendent in his white
front and collar. The band repeated the performance as soon as
they arrived in Bundoran but alas it began to rain and the
whitewash streamed off Soup's collar and front and down his
clothes, much to the amazement of the spectators and the
horror of his fellow bandsmen. Soup fluted away and passed
no remarks.

I'm afraid Soup's culinary genius was his undoing for he
died of food poisoning.

Old Biddy lived near the shore of Lough Erne and visited the
village once a week, probably to collect her five bob a week
pension and some groceries which always included a half
ounce of snuff. She wore men's boots, a long coat and seemed
to have an endless supply of very gay hats decorated with
ribbon and artificial fruit and flowers. Her make-up consisted
of a liberal coating of rouge on her cheeks. As children we
loved to see Biddy arrive in the village. When her shopping
was completed she sat on a window ledge to rest before
embarking on her three mile walk home, while we children
gathered around and listened to her latest adventures with her
numerous imaginary boyfriends. Mr Guttersnipe and Mr
Greengage were two of them. At various intervals she paused
to have a pinch of snuff and this gave her an opportunity to

recharge her imagination. She sang and danced without much persuasion and her favourite songs were Little Brown Jug and Willie Reilly. She made up her dancing to whatever tune she chose to 'la la' and often waltzed to the other side of the village street. Often our school teacher, when introducing a new song at singing lessons, was surprised that we already knew the song for we had learned it from old Biddy of the Lough Shore.

One of our best loved characters was Frandie. Frandie had no fixed abode but slept rough wherever he could, throughout the village and occasionally someone allowed him into the corner of an outhouse when the weather was really bad. He developed bad eyesight early in life and in my memory he had a faint glimmer in one eye and had to use his stick as a guide. He knew everyone in the district, even the children, by the sound of their voice; he was the crier for local auctioneers and travelling shows. These people rehearsed Frandie in what he should shout but invariably he got his words mixed up and shouted the wrong thing and when he became lost for words he rang his bell violently.

Frandie's main occupation was gathering news and gossip from the village and then distributing it around the country-side. He travelled a particular road on the same day each month so that people knew when to expect him; and he only visited houses where he got a good reception by way of a tasty meal and perhaps a gift of eggs and home made bread.

He attended the local Petty Sessions every court day and listened intently to the proceedings and had a remarkable memory; then on his travels he could recite to his hosts who was up at court, the charges, the evidence, the defence, what the Magistrate said, what the witness and the accused said and the fines which were imposed.

The wife of one of our country schoolmasters was a keen botanist. On one occasion she was examining a plant in the hedge on the roadside with her head well into the hedge and her backside next the road. She didn't hear Frandie approach as he felt his way along the road by means of his walking stick. Suddenly Frandie made out through the haze of his small remaining vision, this strange object protruding from the hedge so he raised his stick and gave the lady botanist a hefty whack across her buttocks and at the same time exclaiming 'I never travelled this road yet but there was an ass on it'.

Frandie's brother Johnnie was known as Johnnie the Warrior. He was nick-named 'the Warrior' because his favourite
topic of conversation was war. If there was a major or minor
war taking place in any part of the world Johnnie knew of it
and discussed it to the point of gross exaggeration. As children
we listened intently as he told us of the various campaigns
fought with Germans, Boers, tribesmen and Red Indians.
When he wasn't sure of a nationality or campaign he just
referred to the 'fightin against them blackies'. For years I
thought Johnnie the Warrior was an old soldier but he had
never been out of Fermanagh.

Jemmie and his mother lived in a small thatched cottage at
the back of Drumscambly hill not far from the village. Their
home could be better described as a hovel for they lived, ate
and slept in the one apartment. Jemmie was devoted to his
mother and whatever topic was being discussed he always
related what his mother had said on the subject. 'Will it rain
today Jemmie'? 'Well now, me mother says that it will rain
towards evening'. He was also a singer but never knew a
complete song; he sang what verses he could remember and
then announced 'that's all I know boys, me mother knows the
rest of it'. Jemmie fancied himself as a dancer and like old Biddy
performed dances never seen anywhere before or since. One
of his favourites was 'The Shoemaker's Awl'; this extra-
ordinary dance included jumping and stamping his heavy
nailed boots on the stone flagged floor of some country kitchen. The dance concluded when he sat on the floor and spun
around on his bottom at great speed. Once, while performing
this dance in a neighbour's house, he spun around with such
vigour that his heavy nailed boots collided with a small metal
pot sitting on the hearth stone, smashing it to pieces. The pot,
unfortunately, contained the porridge for supper, some of
which ended up sticking to the wall-paper.

There were many other characters in our neighbourhood
such as Black Barney, Tommy Ned, Charlie the Bee Man, Tom
in the bog, Biddy Allie, McVicker the ragman, Pat Horney, old
Bessie of the dispensary and old Maggie of the back road; all
harmless likeable people who helped add colour to our community.

Outside a Derrygonnelly shop in the 1930s. (Ada Cassidy)

8   Our Shop

CHILDREN who grew up in and around the village in the 1930s didn't spend all their time playing or just wandering. Most of us were required to do a certain amount of work and those who lived on farms were often required to work quite hard.

I was brought up in the environment of a small village grocery shop which was run by my father, who was helped by my mother, two older brothers, shop boys and yard men. My father was also a farmer on a small scale, an undertaker and part-time clerk of the Petty Sessions. He supplied milk to quite a number of the inhabitants of the village who hadn't a milk supply of their own. In a set-up such as this, a boy no matter how young, was given a job to do, if he hadn't the sense to keep a low profile and disappear to some of the many haunts in and around the village.

There is very little comparison between a grocery shop of the 1930s and the modern supermarket of today. One of the first things which struck one on entering an old time grocery shop was the smell, which was very pleasant. It came from a mixture of various foods and spices, for most of the supplies came in bulk and were then filled into paper bags as required. All supplies today are wrapped in various layers of packaging which adds greatly to the price, all in the interest of hygiene. The supermarket has a clinical atmosphere with no chatting or gossiping, just the ring of tills and everyone in a hurry.

Our shop was lit by two large brass lamps suspended from the ceiling, for the local electricity supply was unreliable and expensive. Every morning it was the duty of the shop boys to replenish these with paraffin oil, clean the globes and trim the wicks. There was a counter which ran the full length of the shop and was used for serving customers and making up orders, and parts of it were used for display. Every available square inch of wall was shelved and every shelf was packed to capacity with goods ranging from cornflour to snuff.

My father bought his tea by the chest, which contained one hundred and twelve pounds. It was then filled into one pound, half pound and quarter pound paper bags. Filling, weighing and closing four hundred and forty-eight quarter pound bags of tea, was a long tedious job. Tea came in various categories from what was known as 'good' tea right down to cheap tea. Generally speaking, the poorer people bought the good tea, especially those living in the mountain areas. The cheaper tea was bought by those who were better off, and 'blow ins' also always bought the cheap variety. My father was a good judge of tea and, after a lot of smelling and sniffing, he could mix a special blend which was in good demand.

The same filling, weighing and closing procedure took place for many other commodities such as sugar, currants, raisins, rice, tapioca, baking soda, flour, oatmeal, porridge meal, barley, washing soda and a host of others. All had to be filled by hand or scoop and carefully marked as to their contents in case a customer got washing soda instead of sugar or, worse still, glauber salts! If you spilled or even scattered any on the floor, a sharp slap on the ear was your reward, so that it was wise for a young boy, like myself, to disappear or skidaddle into some of the other centres of activity in the village.

Behind the counter stood a nest of small drawers which contained such varied goods as cloves, nutmeg, cayenne pepper, arrowroot, ginger, cinnamon sticks, caraway seeds, lentils, shoe laces, needles, pins, camphor balls, pen nibs, dummy teats and spectacles. The spectacles were numbered one to sixteen and customers knew the number that suited their eyesight; if they didn't, the complete drawer was set down before them and they tried one set after another while trying to read the local paper.

Just two brands of sweets were stocked, a sticky tough caramel wrapped in paper and boiled sweets which came in little cans. Few of these were actually sold, for a little bag or poke full was put in with each order by way of discount.

At the lower end of the counter, well away from the sunlight from the window, the bacon, butter and lard were kept. The lard was rendered pig fat and came in twenty-eight pound boxes and then weighed to the customers' requirements. There was no mention of polyunsaturated fats, or calories for that matter! The butter fell into two categories, home produced and creamery produced. The bacon was in three categories, slaughterhouse cured, home cured and American. We fattened quite a number of pigs in our back yard. When these were slaughtered the bacon was salted down in large concrete tanks and was eventually sold in the shop. The slaughterhouse bacon was milder and more expensive, while American bacon came from both the USA and Canada packed in large wooden boxes. This bacon was very fat and salty but was the cheapest and was purchased in large pieces of about twelve or fifteen pounds weight; it was either sliced thick for frying or cut off in the piece for boiling. Gallons of bacon oil and lard must have been consumed in our community daily and yet few people died of heart attacks or suffered from pains – perhaps they worked it off and were well lubricated.

Quite a number of people, when they became ill, relied on local cures and charms. When these failed they paid a visit to the shop and surveyed the patent medicine shelf. There was a medicine, a pill or a powder for every ailment known to man. Most treatments began with several spoons of castor oil which was supposed to cure a multitude of ailments. There were cough mixtures, stomach medicines, ointments, camphorated oil, syrup of figs, cascara, glauber salts and an extensive selection of bottles containing various coloured liquids guaranteed to cure any disorder from growing pains to knot on the gut. When all these concoctions failed, only then did they go to the doctor.

On another shelf stood the cattle medicines, Cattline, red drench, worm powders, fluke capsules, embrocation, medicine for red water and hoose, ointments for udders and ringworm, and pellets for black-leg. My father had a reputation for mixing concoctions for both cattle and horses; one famous foul smelling mixture guaranteed the banishment of worms in horses. Like the human beings, treatment of sick animals often began with a charm; if that didn't work then a hefty purgative was concocted which consisted of a mixture of butter, brown sugar, nitre and glauber salts and sometimes treacle. A perfect working bowel seemed to cure most ailments in both man and beast.

Flake tobacco came in one pound and five pound tins. Black bar and twist came in large sealed circular tins and the tobacco was cut off, with a special semi-circular knife, to the customers' requirements. There was also a big demand for snuff, especially amongst the womenfolk. The most popular brands of cigarettes sold were Woodbines, followed by Players and Goldflake.

Most of the weighing up was done in the store adjacent to the shop. Along one wall stood a row of bins containing flour, Indian meal, linseed meal, bran, oats and brown sugar. These items were weighed out in paper bags for customers who didn't require or couldn't afford a complete sack. The paint shelf contained drums of ready mixed orange or blue lead for painting carts as well as a limited selection of ordinary paint. Signal red was a favourite colour for doors and around the hearth fire. Another shelf held soap and candles; there was red, white and carbolic soap for household use and Colleen, a toilet soap for the women folk, also soft soap and saddle soap.

Along the opposite side of the store stood the egg section. Every household in the countryside and some in the village kept hens for egg production which was an important source of income and pin money for the womenfolk. When they were paid for the eggs, by the grocer, they usually had enough money to purchase the week's groceries and of course eggs were an important part of their diet.

They reared all their own hens, swapping settings of eggs with their neighbours so as to avoid close breeding. The cock chickens were fattened and either sold or graced the table for Sunday's dinner or when the clergy were invited for a meal. The old 'laid out' hens were used for making a good pot of soup in the cold weather. The larger farmers, who produced a lot of eggs, brought them to the shop in the horse and cart when going to the creamery, but many housewives, realising that the eggs were their department, chose to carry them in large baskets over their arms and often walked several miles to the village with their heavy cumbersome load.

My mother always kept a large pot of tea brewing on the old black range so that these ladies could have a refreshing cup of tea, often called a 'squib', and a rest before returning home with their baskets heavily laden again with groceries.

The eggs were then sent to the packing station where they were tested and packed in large boxes lined with straw and dispatched to the railway station in Enniskillen and thence to Liverpool and Glasgow.

Further down the store stood the boot, shoe and leather department. There were heavy nailed 'Clarke's' boots, slightly lighter sparible boots and kip or soft Sunday boots. There were also women's boots, both heavy and light, which laced up above the ankle. Few shoes were stocked as they were in little demand. Those who were fashion conscious went to Enniskillen to do their footwear shopping. The leather was sold by weight and consisted of various thicknesses for soles and uppers and was chiefly purchased by the many cobblers in the district.

Just off the store stood the oil house. Large quantities of paraffin were sold for kitchen and hurricane lamps, and candles were sold to provide light in the bedrooms. Lubricating oil and grease were purchased for mowing machines and cart axles, while paint oil and linseed oil was bought for mixing with orange lead for painting carts. All these oils came in drums or barrels and were measured out into bottles.

When a customer arrived with a long shopping list it took some time to make up the order as many items had to be filled or measured out, so they amused themselves by chatting to each other. There was no self service in those days. It was also the task of the shopkeeper to stimulate these conversations and encourage the customers to keep the discussions going by intervening from time to time with a few well chosen remarks. This ensured that the customer didn't become bored while waiting.

My father was part-time Clerk of the Petty Sessions for the area and used part of our front room as his office. The court sat once every month in the courthouse which was situated at the lower end of the village. At the entrance to this building there were four steps, so if you were seen doing something wrong which might be against the law such as kicking a ball on the street, someone might shout 'Hey boy, you'll find yourself up the steps'.

Our police in the village were always very active and some of the villagers found themselves in court for very minor and trivial misdemeanours. There was a continuous campaign against cycling offences such as bad brakes, no bell, riding a cycle during the hours of darkness without a front light or reflector, carrying a passenger on a bicycle or turning a corner on the wrong side. All these offences attracted a fine of two shillings with one shilling costs. There were also charges for driving a horse or ass and cart without due care and attention and if the owner didn't have his name and address clearly painted on his cart, he was prosecuted. Other more serious crimes were cattle wandering on the public highway and having unlicensed dogs. Playing football or handball on the village street was also sure to send one 'up the steps'.

My father wrote out the summonses which were served by the policemen. He also 'swore in' the accused and witnesses and recorded the verdicts.

The local court attracted many spectators and occasionally the press from Enniskillen; together with the accused, witnesses and maybe a solicitor or two, the courthouse was usually packed.

Crimes of theft were not very common and vandalism was non-existent, although it was surprising the number of people who were brought to court for being drunk and disorderly.

Maud Hamilton, Elsie Parke, Hugh Dundas, Olive Irwin and Willie Parke.

9   Our Back Yard

I KEPT well away from both shop and store because one minute I received a sharp slap on the ear from my parents or a member of staff for standing in the way, the next minute I was given a boring job or sent on a message. I spent many hours, however, in the yard with the men and animals. The staff who worked in the yard seemed to have more patience and always found time to talk and tell me all kinds of tales regarding ghosts and fairies. They also taught me how to look after cattle, how to drive a horse properly and how to milk a cow.

You entered our yard from the village street through an archway and it stretched right down to the river bank. The building nearest the shop contained light hardware such as nails, basins, tin baths, porringers, saucepans, metal pots and pans, kettles and skillets. It also contained farm implements such as spades, graipes, shovels, turf spades, rope, scythes, grasshooks and many other everyday household and farm items.

The building alongside was the hearse house. The hearse was always covered with a large sheet in order to protect it from dust and bird droppings. The birds, such as pigeons and sparrows, frequented the stores in search of meal. Along one side of the building, also covered, were coffins of all sizes and qualities from heavy panelled oak to plain soft wood. The hearse harness was hung carefully on special pegs and on a shelf nearby, cardboard boxes containing coffin lining, handles, breast plates, shrouds, stockings, tassels and screws, were neatly stacked.

Further down stood a large meal store which contained cattle food from various parts of the world. There were no compounds in those days. The farmer purchased the meal as 'straights' and then compounded his own mixture for cattle or pigs. The most popular was yellow meal or Indian meal which came in various brands such as Roller Cut and Easy Burst and in eight or sixteen stone sacks. Other meals were flaked or cooked maize which sold under the brand name of Clarendo, also pollard, bran, linseed meal, oat meal, fish meal and oats. Flour came in eight stone and four stone packs and the common brands were Five Star, Millocrat and Early Riser. The empty packs were saved by the housewife, ripped out flat and washed, then several were sewn together and used as bed sheets. There was a servant boy in our area who found it difficult to leave his bed in the morning. One morning the farmer lost patience, dragged the young man out of bed and pointing to the bed sheet he exclaimed 'What do you see printed on that sheet boy? Early Riser. How can ye bear to lie on that to this time of the mornin?' The local football team had their shorts made out of flour packs and when the team took the field they invariably had Early Riser or Five Star emblazoned on their backsides.

The loft above the meal store was known as the tea loft and it was here that chests of tea were stored and it was also used to store spare grocery supplies, together with wrapping paper, string, paper bags and many other bits and pieces associated with the grocery trade.

Further down the yard stood the stables where we always kept a least two draught horses and a driving horse or pony. These animals were used for delivering the cattle feed, drawing the hearse and farm work. We didn't have a car so the driving horse was used for pulling the trap when visiting or attending our place of worship.

Nearby stood the byre which contained a herd of milking cows. The loft above was where the hay was stored, while alongside was a large lean-to-shed for the carts, spring carts and an assortment of harness. Further down again stood a row of small houses for pigs and small calves, some fowl coops and a large manure pit known as the 'ducal'. Bordering the river was a small vegetable and flower garden, and last but not least, a small building, commonly known as a closet, which protruded over the river. We had no piped water supply or flush toilets in those days so that this little building over the river was where we went to relieve ourselves hoping that some adventurous boy playing in the river didn't interrupt our pleasure with a poke of a stick on the posterior.

The creamery operated six days a week except during the winter months, when milk was in short supply and it operated for three. The farmers delivered their milk to the creamery in the morning. Then they drove down the village street to their particular grocery shop where they delivered their eggs and collected a supply of cattle feed and groceries. Some of them then liked a pint or two of porter. If a young boy was standing around he was often asked to hold the horse until the farmer returned. The reward was usually a halfpenny or maybe a penny from the more generous, but sometimes it was just a pat on the head and maybe the remark 'You're a great cub, so ye are'. Some horses were quiet and docile and stood half asleep in the same spot on the village street for hours. One local farmer, who had a reputation for being absent minded, drove his horse and cart to Enniskillen. He chatted with friends, completed his business and then set off for home on the bus, completely forgetting that he came with his horse and cart. It was only when he arrived home that he remembered and set off back to Enniskillen, this time by bicycle, to find the old horse exactly where he had left him.

The village was a very busy place in the mornings during creamery time, when both sides of the village street were lined with horses and carts as well as pony and ass carts and spring carts. We seldom saw a car or a lorry and if one appeared there was a stampede of farmers to their animals, in case they became scared and ran away, which might result in serious damage. The drivers of the infernal machines were cursed from one end of the village to the other, for scaring a horse was an unpardonable sin.

In the afternoons, both our horses and spring carts were sent out with their drivers to deliver cattle feed to farmers in the surrounding area. We had three yard men, Joe, Willie and Barney and I usually travelled with one of them and they allowed me to drive the horse. Joe was considered to be a good handler of a horse and when he let me drive I had to do it properly. He taught me a lot about horses such as how to make the harness fit properly. He encouraged me to sleek the animals and talk to them and not to chuck the reins needlessly and risk damaging their mouths. All these little tips, together with experience, were aimed at making me 'a good handler of a horse'. These characteristics often came naturally to some people and never to others. I have known horses to become agitated just by the sound of a particular person's voice and to be comforted by others.

At some farms we were invited in for tea. I well remember one particular farmhouse up in the mountain area where we were always sat down to a mug of strong tea, a freshly laid, boiled egg and a large slice of home-made fadge bread. The taste of those meals has lingered with me ever since as the food was very welcome after a long sit on a cart on a cold day. Fadge is homemade bread baked on the hearth in a pot oven or on a griddle with either flour or oaten meal. It is delicious served hot and smothered in butter.

My father was an accomplished horseman and was very particular about the welfare of his animals. He ensured that after work they were well rubbed down, properly watered, fed and bedded down. He had a beautiful rubber tyred trap for his half bred mare and a set of brown silver mounted harness. The entire combination was a beautiful turnout. He didn't own a car, he couldn't even drive one and this was his mode of transport when going to church, attending funerals or visiting. What could be more exhilarating than sitting in a trap behind a good trotting horse on a good day travelling around our beautiful countryside?

It was on this mare that I was taught to ride by Jackie, a famous horseman from Enniskillen. Many years later I found myself acting as an animal transport officer when serving near the North West Frontier in India when Jackie's tuition stood me in good stead and Joe's instruction on patience and proper handling helped me immensely when struggling with obstinate mules. I remember, when training, a small pompous officer with a large moustache and a monocle, asked us how we knew the difference between a horse and a mare. My hand shot up immediately 'Look under its tail', I replied; 'Nonsense' he said 'Much too vulgar, you look in its mouth'. I suppose he was right but I doubt if anyone around Derrygonnelly would agree.

Every Saturday we operated a travelling shop covering a round trip of about twenty miles through a mainly remote mountainous region. The travelling shop consisted of a four wheeled vehicle very similar to a covered wagon or prairie schooner and was hauled by two horses. We collected the eggs from the womenfolk who in turn purchased their groceries, cigarettes, tobacco, patent medicines and other supplies for they lived far from the village shops which they only visited occasionally. The following Monday we returned with animal feed, packs of flour, paraffin oil and any other special order that wasn't on board on Saturday. The wagon set out around 10 o'clock in the morning and returned about 10 o'clock at night.

When someone in the neighbourhood died, the news travelled quickly and the locals rallied around the bereaved and shared their grief at the same time offering any assistance required. Many preparations were put in hand such as ordering supplies for the wake, procuring extra seating for the callers, contacting the clergy and the undertaker and arranging the day and time of the funeral. The immediate neighbours gave their assistance by looking after livestock, cooking food, helping at the wake and digging the grave.

The close relations of the deceased came to our shop to order the coffin, hearse and supplies for the wake. They always came in pairs, I expect to give each other moral support when making decisions. My father knew, from experience, what was needed; bread, butter, tea, sugar, candles, jam, cigarettes, tobacco, snuff, matches and cordial. Whiskey was purchased in the public house for the menfolk and port wine for the womenfolk while those who were teetotal drank cordial.

My father then enquired in a discreet manner what quality of coffin they required. Very often, in their grief, they were inclined to be over-extravagant and replied 'The best of everything Charlie' – in other words they wanted an oak coffin adorned with elaborate handles, breast plate, tassels and lined with expensive material. The breast plate bore the full name of the deceased, date of death and their age. There was an awful rumpus if the wrong details were put on the breast plate as most people in the area knew each other's age. 'She's far more than that for I sat next to her at school' someone might mumble at the graveside.

As soon as the funeral arrangements were finalised our yard staff went into action for there was a lot to do and time was short. The hearse was pushed out to the yard where it was uncovered, washed and when dry, polished. My job, because I was small, was polishing the inside which included the glass, silver mounted rails and stoppers. The harness was, of course, black, very ornate with silver coloured mountings and had many more straps than necessary just for decoration. The leather was blackened with bootpolish and rubbed until it shone. The mountings were then polished with metal polish and it was a serious matter to allow the metal polish to stain the leather. I always tried to steer clear of the hearse harness for it was a boring, exacting task to clean it.

In the meantime the two black horses had their tails and manes pulled, followed by a thorough wash all over with warm water and soft soap. When the animals dried, their coats were rubbed down with a soft dry cloth until they shone. The last task before they were yoked to the hearse was to clean their hooves and paint them with black oil. We always kept black horses, if at all possible, for they looked better drawing a hearse than any other colour. If an undertaker used a light chestnut, a white or a piebald, he was out of business right away.

The coffin was prepared as soon as possible and brought to the wake house where the deceased was coffined. It was important to choose the proper length of the coffin; if it was too short the body wouldn't fit; if it was too long the body slid around when the coffin was carried. In order to avoid such a catastrophe and short of actually measuring the corpse, some-one was found who was approximately the size of the corpse and he were either measured or put into the coffin. Tuberculo-sis was a scourge and common cause of death in those days, especially amongst the young, so occasionally I was the one who was put in the coffin for measuring.

The coffin was first lined with a coat of pitch, followed by a layer of shavings or fine hay. It was then lined with special white and purple material and finished off with a top covering cloth and pillow. Finally the handles, breast plate, lid screws and tassels were put on and the job was completed and ready for delivery to the wake house. Here the body was reverently coffined and the neighbours and friends filed into the room to view, say a prayer and often remark 'Isn't he looking well?' or 'He's powerful like himself'.

The houses in those days were quite small and every available space was taken up by visitors and callers. It was a trying time for the bereaved, for they had no hope of being able to express their grief in private.

On the day of the funeral the hearse was steered on to the village street, properly to show it off and then the horses in all their splendour were led out and hitched. Joe, dressed in his black coat and tall silk hat, climbed on to the driving seat and off they clattered up the village street on their way to the home of the deceased, with the villagers and shoppers looking on in admiration and reverence. A village wit might remark 'Everyone is dying to get a ride in that thing'.

Motorcars were few in those days and many travelled to funerals by horse and trap, side car or jaunting car. The remainder walked, some wheeling bicycles so that they could cycle home.

The cows were driven from the fields into the byre and milked twice a day at seven thirty in the morning and five thirty in the evening. We all took an occasional hand at this task but it was mainly done by the yardmen and servant girl. During the winter the cows remained in the byre and were let out briefly at mid-day to drink at the mill race, lick themselves and scratch against anything rough and solid. During the summer months they were grazed in various fields around the village. The byre was kept scrupulously clean and the mucking out took place twice daily. The walls were whitewashed and tarred regularly. The milk was brought up to the little dairy where it was strained into earthenware crocks to cool before it was distributed to customers. Those were the days before milk bottles came to the village and the milk was distributed morning and evening in little tin or enamelled cans which held either a pint or a quart.

Delivering milk was a task I detested, especially in the mornings when I wanted to spend my limited time before school revising my tables or spellings. It was also extremely cold on my hands carrying two cans of milk in each with the wire handles cutting into my fingers. It wasn't so bad in the evenings, for there was no rush and I took time to chat in some of the houses. We delivered a pint and a half of milk every morning to a school teacher known as 'the waterhen'. This lady lived alone and was a fairly heavy smoker. It was also obvious that she ate a fry every morning for breakfast, mostly using her fingers instead of a knife and fork, for when she opened the door just wide enough to let in the can, still wearing her nightie, she stuck out her finger covered with nicotine and bacon oil and I hung the can of milk on it.

My last call in the evening delivery was to an old lady who lived at the lower entrance to the village. Her kitchen was small, neat and warm with a cheery fire burning in a little black range. Her late husband had been a regular soldier and she travelled to several foreign stations with him during his ser-vice. I was invited to sit on a little stool in front of the fire surrounded by mementos of her army travels while she regaled me with fascinating stories about the exploits of her husband and his regiment.

Other customers called for their own supply of milk and carried it home in a sweetie can. Boiled sweets such as brandy balls and bull's eyes came packed in tin cans and, when emptied, these were much sought after for holding milk and carrying tea to the working men in the fields. The travelling tinkers or tin smiths also made an assortment of utensils such as porringers and cans.

I was introduced to milking cows at an early age. A beginner first of all was confined to stripping; this was a procedure where you went around the cows that were already milked to make sure there was no milk left in the udder in order to avoid damage caused by bacteria. Milk from strippings was reputed to be the best for tea. The beginner was then allowed to start on a quiet cow and one which was easy to milk.

Most milk in the area was produced during the summer months when there was a good flush of grass and when meal was not required. Our supply of milk had to be kept up all the year round and often my father had to purchase a newly calved cow during the winter when they were scarce and expensive as the natural time to calve was in the spring.

Many farmers, and even householders who had an acre or so around their house, not only kept laying hens to supplement their income, but many reared a flock of turkeys for the Christmas market.

Turkeys are delicate birds and difficult to rear, especially if their accommodation is cold and draughty. Nevertheless these folk were very experienced and when Christmas approached they had a flock of ten or twelve turkeys for sale which brought in some welcome extra cash for the festive season.

At the beginning of December, preparations were made for the killing and plucking of hundreds of turkeys and one of the large stores in the yard was cleaned and benches set up around the walls for the pluckers to sit on. The birds were purchased from the producers by weight and the price per pound often fluctuated from day to day. The hens usually weighed from around nine to twelve pounds while the cocks were fourteen to eighteen. During the 1930s the prices were from five pence to eight pence per pound.

The plucking commenced at about seven o'clock in the evening and went on well into the night; this carried on for about a fortnight. It was an opportunity for young farm workers and shop assistants also to earn some extra cash for Christmas, for it was they who performed this onerous and boring work.

Killing a turkey by breaking its neck was a job for the expert. A strong rope was suspended from the ceiling with a loop at the end. The bird's legs were inserted into the loop and with a smart twist and pull on its neck, life was extinct in a split second. The dead birds were then distributed to the pluckers who sat on the benches. Here again the task had to be done properly, cleanly and quickly, making sure that the skin wasn't damaged or torn. Each plucker was given two turkeys at a time and when they were completed he brought them up to the table to be inspected and entered to his credit in the book. The pay was two pence per bird.

The birds were then hung in a cool building before they were dispatched to the shipper and thence to the English or Scottish markets. The boring task of plucking was often interrupted by a bit of horse play, such as throwing armfuls of feathers over each other, or maybe someone told a good yarn or two. When a plucker finished his first turkey he put it under his bench keeping his foot on its neck in case one of the other lads pinched it.

In the late nineteenth century an attempt was made to connect Derrygonnelly with Enniskillen by rail, similar to the Clogher Valley Railway which ran along the side of the road. There were many objections to the scheme and the main one was that the train would scare the horses travelling along the road. It was never built and the horse reigned supreme in Derrygonnelly for many years after.

In the late 1920s, attempts were made to speed things up as all our supplies were brought by horse and cart from the railway station at Enniskillen, a distance of ten miles. A local merchant purchased a steam lorry which carried one and a half tons; I just remember this ungainly vehicle puffing up the village street in a cloud of smoke and vapour. If ever a vehicle was designed to scare horses, this was it. The wheels were shod with solid rubber and as those were the days before tarmacadam, the steam lorry often sank into the muddy road surface and was hauled out by horses. My father, not to be outdone, purchased a one ton Traffic petrol driven lorry also with solid tyres. Its registration number was IL 634 so it must have been registered around 1924 and it went off the road in 1931. Both these vehicles went off the road around the same time and for another few years we went back to the horse and cart. I remember my father sending men with horses and carts carrying cases of eggs to the railway station and returning with coal, meal and grocery supplies; so transport seemed to have a temporary set-back around this period. He also purchased a horse-drawn coach from the proprietor of the Royal Hotel in Enniskillen as he had the contract for transporting the children from the shore road area to the schools in the village.

The introduction of the pneumatic tyre for vehicles, an Ulster invention, brought immediate changes to the village, a bus service began, a local man started a taxi service and another purchased a two-ton lorry for hauling goods to and from Enniskillen. The old nag, however, continued on the farm for the next twenty years when tractors eventually took over.

As time went by lorries became larger, their engines more

powerful and reliable, and soon they were by-passing the railways and hauling direct from Belfast and Londonderry.

In 1936 my father purchased a four ton Commer lorry and Joe's brother, Harry, was employed to drive it. This opened up a whole new world for me as I went to Belfast and Londonderry for the first time in my life. We left home around six o'clock in the morning when going to Belfast and, provided we didn't encounter any mishaps, we arrived around ten o'clock. We drove straight to Green's or Marshall's meal mills where we collected the various types of meal. Harry was an expert at building the bags so that they were secure, for the road through the Clogher Valley was very winding and a load could easily fall apart. After the four ton of meal was collected, Harry set off around the wholesale houses where he collected supplies of groceries, household and farm implements and items of hardware. These supplies were placed in a hollow in the bags on top of the load and if the weather was wet a large canvas cover was tied on. Calling at wholesale houses was very time-consuming so that it could be three o'clock in the afternoon before we set off for home, travelling at a much slower speed than when empty. We were very lucky if we arrived home by eight o'clock. The lorry then had to be unloaded as it would probably be required to go to Derry the following morning.

Unloading the lorry at night was not a problem; a number of young men, some unemployed, others farm workers, congregated at the street corner and waited patiently for the load to arrive and in return for a packet of Woodbine cigarettes each, carried the sacks of meal into the meal store by the light of hurricane lamps.

Next morning the lorry set off for Derry and if a coal boat was unloading, Harry drove to Lane's Wharf where the lorry was loaded straight from the boat by means of a large bucket on a crane.

Looking down into the hold of the coal boat I saw the four navvies shovelling coal into the bucket at lightning speed; at a given signal they stood back for a rest and four others took their place. In a short time the lorry was loaded, weighed and ready for home. There were also meal mills in Derry at Christie's and I.A.W.S., the Irish Agricultural Wholesale Society.

The journey was much shorter than to Belfast and was shorter still if we took the road over Scraghy Mountain but this route tended to be treacherous during winter.

We had a set of crates made for the lorry so that cattle could be transported. This was a great relief to me for I must have walked and run what seemed like hundreds of miles driving cattle. This also did away with the five hour walk with cattle to Enniskillen fair. I didn't mind this walk because I got a day off school but if we didn't sell the cattle I didn't look forward to the ten miles walk home which was heartbreaking.

We never owned a motor car until my brother bought a little Morris Eight in 1943. My father never learned to drive, preferring to travel around the countryside by means of his beloved horse and trap.

Haymaking in Fermanagh in the 1930s.

10   Farming

THE GROCERS in our village liked to describe themselves as merchants, because of the diversity of their business and most of it was done with farmers or small holders. It was surprising the number of people in both village and countryside, who owned just an acre or two, kept a cow and calf and put in a little crop.

The first three months of the year were the most trying for the farmer; cattle generally were in poor condition, income was non- existent, meal was expensive and in many cases cash flow dried up altogether. One would think that the obvious thing for a farmer to do under these circumstances was to sell some of his cattle. Unfortunately that was easier said than done for a cattle dealer didn't want cattle in poor condition; so the farmer often turned to his merchant, to whom he probably owed money anyway, to ease his financial problem by taking some cattle off his hands whether they were in good condition or not. It was therefore essential that the merchant owned or rented land in order to operate this barter or exchange service.

My father owned a little land but rented quite a number of acres here and there around the district and from time to time found himself with quite a number of cattle in poor condition. However, he was pretty good at cattle management, for with good food and some of his medical concoctions they mostly turned out well, especially after a summer's grass. I often wondered, at that time, why he never bought more land as it was quite cheap in the 1930s but it never dawned on me that he just hadn't the money, because it took substantial cash flow, even in a small village, to buy the stock for the shop, purchase cattle and give credit in difficult times.

Our herd of milk cows was grazed in fields near the village

and was driven in to be milked twice a day. The land for the young cattle was scattered here and there and as there were no such things as cattle lorries or tractor trailers, they were driven along the road from one farm to the other and also to the cattle fair. Cattle driving was a skill that was acquired by practice and much abuse from one's elders.

Cattle driving was really a job for two people and because I was young and quite fleet of foot, I did most of the running. There were many things to remember. One was that cattle are always inclined to run back to where they came from, if given the chance. Farmers who left gates and field gaps open along the roadside caused a lot of trouble to the cattle drover and it was my job to run and close them before the cattle arrived. It was inadvisable to strike the animals with our sticks, if at all possible, as it upset them; so as long as they were going in the right direction we left them alone. Some people liked striking cattle and such behaviour was not only cruel, but it upset them so that they separated in all directions. A good drover should be able to anticipate if the cattle are going to do the wrong thing and then beat them to it as quietly as possible.

It was important to inspect the cattle on the different farms each day and country boys were taught from an early age to do this job carefully. I found it very pleasant setting out early in the morning to perform this task. The first thing to do was – stand well away from the cattle and count them. One or two could have strayed or maybe one was sick and lying alone in another field. Approach them slowly and, as the old timers used to say, 'Check if they were all doing something'. If they were grazing, chewing their cud or licking themselves, then they were all right. If a beast was standing still and alone it required closer attention. The most common ailments were red water and black leg and others were chill, tummy upset, constipation or timber tongue or maybe the fairies put a spell on them. Sometimes a known individual in the community had the power to 'Put a blink on an animal'. It was also very important to inspect the fences and water supply.

It took an enormous quantity of hay to fodder the young cattle, horses and milk cows during the winter months and the harvesting of the hay crop was backbreaking work, especially during inclement weather. Because we had so much ground to cover, good haymaking machinery was essential. We had a two-horse Deering mowing machine, a Pierce hayraking machine, a tedding machine and a tumbling paddy, together with an assortment of hayforks and rakes. Smaller farmers had a one-horse mowing machine and the remaining work was done by hand rake and fork. The smallholder, and there were many of these, cut their hay with a scythe which was really slavish work. A good man could mow an acre a day with a scythe but this left him with little time or energy for anything else. There were men in the area who were considered experts and they mowed day after day during the haymaking season. In order to keep this up it was essential that they had a good blade and the purchasing and selecting was a long drawn out procedure. This was done by hitting the blade against a stone and listening to the ring. The colour and thickness of the metal was also taken into consideration. The blade was then turned by the local blacksmith to a suitable angle to suit the mower. The handle or snead was selected or sometimes just cut out of the hedge. Two handles were next attached to the snead and fitted in relation to the mower's height, the length of arms and his usual stance when mowing. It was essential that a mower should be capable of putting a good edge on the blade, otherwise he tired very soon. The sharpening process was done with two qualities of sharpening stone, one rough and one smooth. A good sharpener could put on an edge like a lance using a local Kilty stone manufactured in Kiltyclogher.

When the hay was cut it was allowed to stay in the swathe for about two days and then turned with hand rakes. After another day it was tedded and, if the weather remained fair, was wind-rowed and finally gathered in with a horse and tumbling paddy and built into rucks. At any time during this operation it might rain and the whole operation had to be repeated when it faired.

During a wet summer a farmer spent weeks trying to save one field of hay and he entered the winter with inferior fodder and not enough of it, resulting in poorly fed cattle. It also meant that he had to purchase extra meal, thus depleting his already meagre income.

The hay was left in the rucks to season for about three weeks and then stored for the winter. The larger farmers had hay-sheds for storing but many built their hay in haystacks or pikes. The haystacks were built near the farm buildings while the smaller round pikes could be seen on different parts of the farm where cattle were outwintered. Both were thatched with rushes and tied down with hay rope or Hairy Ned which was cheap rope made from rough brown fibre.

Building a haystack was a trade in itself and the work was directed by whoever was the expert in the area. He supervised the building, dressing and placing of the greeshoch or final covering of green grass on top. We didn't have a hayshed, so all our hay was either stacked or piked where it was saved and then during the winter was transported into the lofts in the yard as it was needed. Our director of operations around the haystack was Joe's father, Jemmie, who also did the thatching.

Building hay on a cart was a task for the expert who could slope the load over the horse almost as far as his ears and also to the rear, thus putting twice as much hay on the cart. The land in our area was not suitable for producing grain crops, so hay was our principal cattle food apart from the odd farmer who grew turnips.

The gestation period of a cow is just over nine months and when calving time approached we watched for the tell-tale signs. These signs were when the udder sprang and filled with colostrum or beastings and the calf bones in the pelvis went down. At this point a strict eye was kept on the animal in case she got into difficulties when calving commenced. Sometimes the cow needed assistance and occasionally the calf was dead, the wrong way round or legs and head down, in which case expert help was called in quickly. There were a number of cow doctors in the area who had no qualifications whatsoever but vast experience and skill, probably handed down through several generations; so one was called if needed as our nearest veterinary surgeon was ten miles away.

Farmers always reared their calves, keeping the best heifer calves for cow replacements and the others were sold at various stages depending on the farmer's acreage or if he owned an 'out' farm. We always sold our newly born calves when about ten days old as we had not the facilities to rear them. I invariably got the time consuming job of feeding the young calves. It was natural for a young calf to suck; so it was a task of patience to teach it to drink out of a bucket instead but with lots of practice I became quite an expert.

We fattened about ten pigs at a time in two lots of five each. These were bought in at around twelve weeks old and after about another fifteen weeks were ready for slaughter.

Most households in both country and village kept pigs; any number from one to ten at a time, depending on the accommodation available. Most people fattened just two pigs and they were fed quite cheaply on small potatoes, any other food left over from mealtimes, skim milk and a little meal. It was inadvisable to keep just one pig as these animals have little hair and will not thrive if they are cold; two pigs keep each other warm. The small pig houses were often built against the gable wall of the dwelling house, especially if the fireplace was behind it.

When two pigs were slaughtered, one was salted down for household use in a large barrel or wooden box. After some time the bacon was taken out and hung from the kitchen ceiling in the vicinity of the hearth fire. It was thus dried out and given a beautiful smoked flavour. This bacon was used for breakfast, dinner and tea; sliced for frying, cut in a piece for boiling and served with vegetables which were sometimes fried in the bacon grease. The other carcass was brought to the market and sold to a pork buyer. There was always an urgent need waiting for the pig money, such as the Land Annuity rent to the government or clothes for the children.

We usually slaughtered five pigs at a time and the task was one that I didn't relish; so I kept away as far as possible from the gory operation. There were a number of men in the area who were expert slaughtermen and who also did the cutting up and salting. We employed an old fellow named Phil who never stopped talking while he worked and spoke with great wisdom on most subjects and never tired blowing his own trumpet.

Early on the appropriate day the fire in the old range was well stoked up, for gallons of boiling water were required. A low bench or platform made from a door supported by wooden egg boxes was erected at the lower end of the yard. At the end of the bench stood a large wooden tub of boiling water. The first victim was hauled out by the ears and tail and when in the proper position Phil wielded a large wooden mallet, hitting the unsuspecting animal between the eyes. As the animal collapsed he grabbed his knife, already honed to perfection, and deftly slit the pig's throat. Blood splattered all over the place while the helpers waited until they were sure the animal had shed the last drop. The carcass was then heaved on to the bench and the front half was immersed in the tub of boiling water, enabling the bristly hair to be scraped off; this was repeated on the other half and soon it was clean and snow white. It was then hung up from a beam by the heels and the belly was slit open from tail to head and the contents tumbled out. Guts, lungs, heart, spleen, liver and bladder all fell to the floor. The young boys of the village congregated not only to watch the proceedings but also to commandeer the bladders, which were washed, blown up and used as footballs.

After a few days the carcasses were really stiff and Phil returned to cut and bone them out ready for salting. A mixture of salt and nitre was rubbed into the pork and it was then placed in a large concrete tank in order to mature into bacon. When the bacon was ready it was taken out and sold in the shop.

On the west side of the village the land consisted of bog where the villagers cut their turf. When part of the bog was exhausted, 'cut out' as we put it, the plots were reclaimed and were excellent for growing potatoes and grazing a cow or an ass. Over the years almost every householder in the village owned a plot of land on the outskirts. The system was handed down from the times when the landlord let every tenant have turbary or turf-cutting rights somewhere on his estate.

We had various systems of valuation for farms over the centuries but in our area, and I'm sure in many others, we had our own unofficial system handed down through the generations; it was that of the 'cow's place'. This meant that if a farm was described as eight cow's place it would support eight cows, eight young calves and a horse. The calves were usually sold as year-olds to make way for the next crop, only keeping a heifer calf out of a good cow. It obviously took more bad land to support the eight cows and more still if it was mountainous.

The mountain farmer had lots of turf bog on his own land; so he hadn't far to travel to cut his turf. Some of the lowland farmers travelled as far as seven miles to cut turf and could only draw home one load a day. The mountain farmer, on the other hand, cut far more turf than he needed. So every time he came to the village for a bag or two of meal, he brought a load of turf with him and sold it to a villager and the money helped pay for the meal. The sale of young cattle, the fat pig, eggs, a few cock chickens, a flock of turkeys and the odd crate of turf – all helped to keep the small farmer's head above water.

To the farming community in the 1930s the fair days were still very important. To the present day generation a fair means roundabouts, swing boats and dodgem cars, candy floss and big dippers but to the older people it means a different thing entirely. A fair in bygone days was where the farmers bought and sold their animals. In other words, it was a market.

Derrygonnelly fair was held on the twenty-fourth of each month and it depended on the time of year whether the fair was big or small. The April, June and July fairs were quite big as the large graziers 'bought in' for the summer's grass while the smaller farmer sold young cattle in order to save grass for his cows and to accommodate another younger lot. The September, October and November fairs were also quite big when farmers cut down their numbers for the winter. Cattle had to be sold sometime, but the timing was important for that helped determine the price. The condition of the animals also made a difference to demand and value. Cattle from the Derrygonnelly area were always in good demand as they were both hardy and healthy and they thrived well when put on good land after coming off the mountains and blue clay hills of our area. We had just two breeds, Shorthorn and Aberdeen Angus; those were the days before the Hereford, Friesian and Continental breeds were introduced.

The evening before the fair, cattle dealers arrived in the village and spent the night in lodgings so that they were out early the next morning to meet the droves of cattle; that way they had first pick. Around eight thirty the first cattle began to arrive and every road leading to the village was packed with animals of all ages and sizes. They made their way to the fair green at the rear of the village but often it didn't hold them all, so they occupied several approach roads as well. Along the road leading to the village street were lines of horse carts containing young pigs for sale, sheaves of rye straw for thatch, scollops or sally and hazel rods for holding down the thatch, cabbage plants and maybe one containing young coniferous trees which the farmers often planted for shelter belts around their dwellings.

The shopkeepers of the village made an extra effort on the fair day by stocking up and displaying some of their wares on the sidepath in front of their shops – ready made suits, suit lengths, farm hand tools and implements, new and second hand bicycles, heavy farm boots, turf spades, McMahon and Patterson spades, meal and various other farm and household articles.

Many 'cants' or stalls were set up on the sidepath selling second hand clothes, rope, tools and crockery. Shooting galleries, dart throwing, rickety wheels and crown and anchor stalls did a roaring trade. Travelling musicians, playing fiddles, or melodeons, and street singers rendered many old favourites and passed around the cap. Strong men balanced twenty foot ladders and cart wheels on their chins and others allowed themselves to be tied up with chains and then wriggled out of them. A troupe of coloured gentlemen often came and performed a tribal dance and lay bare backed on a bed of nails or broken glass.

I rather liked herding cattle at the fair for I got a day off school: anyway I enjoyed the bargaining and haggling and there was always something going on. I knew many cattle dealers by sight; those who bought for shipping and arrived at the price fairly quickly and also there was the dealer who travelled from one fair to another looking for the odd bargain. There were some dealers who walked through your little herd of cattle scattering them all over the place and then bid a ridiculous price, or they might bid for one animal when you wanted to sell all of them together.

There were cattle dealers who specialised in particular types of cattle. Some only purchased springing or calved cows and heifers whilst others bought old worn out cows or mincers for the Glasgow mince and sausage trade, and others wanted calves or stirks or store bullocks.

The seller asked a few pounds each more than he was prepared to take, the dealer offered a few pounds less and so the bargaining began. Other farmers and dealers joined the scene, and everytime a bid was made they slapped hands and when the asking price was reduced they slapped again. This went on until the final price was agreed and the slap was accompanied by a spit on the hand in order to seal the bargain and settle on the 'luck penny'. The dealer then put his private mark on the cattle with either a keel marker or a pair of scissors and they were driven into an enclosed yard where all the sold cattle were kept.

Some farmers were never satisfied with the prices they were offered and brought their cattle home again to return with them the following fair. In fact this could happen for several fairs until the cattle knew their own way to the fair and home again.

In the evening drovers set off with the purchased cattle to the railway station at Enniskillen ten miles away, bound for the Belfast docks and the Birkenhead or Glasgow cattle boat. The cattle dealer stood at a particular pre-arranged place and time where he paid for the cattle, always in cash.

The hiring fairs were held on the twenty fourth of May and the twenty fourth of November. The May hiring was the more important for it was then that the men were hired for the summer's work. The men and girls who were offering themselves for hire stood around on the footpath at a particular part of the street. The men fell into different categories. There was the top class man who could work a pair of horses and a mowing machine, and was a good milker, knowledgeable with cattle, an early riser and clean. This type of man demanded the top hiring wage and could afford a certain amount of latitude in choosing his employer. Others fell into lower categories right down to the young boy just left school or the man who required constant supervision. These men received a low wage and at times found it difficult to secure a hiring, often being forced to emigrate.

During the 1930s a top man received around twenty pounds for the summer six months together with food and lodging and around fifteen pounds for winter. The lower bracket might be ten or seven pounds. The girls were hired either by so much a month or the whole six months and their wages fluctuated from one pound fifty to two pounds a month, together with food and lodgings.

Some farmers, who had the name of serving inferior food or providing bad accommodation, or maybe demanding that a man worked longer hours than usual, found it difficult to hire a good man. There were also farmers who had inferior equipment or lived in a remote area and they also found difficulty in hiring people.

The hired men took a few days holiday at hiring time. They also got holy days, the twelfth of July and Sundays off but the milking, foddering and cleaning out was done before they left. They worked a twelve hour day from about seven thirty in the morning to seven thirty in the evening except during the hay saving time when, if the weather was good, they might work until midnight. They worked six days a week, together with the essential work on Sundays and overtime pay was unheard of.

The wages might seem small but profits in farming at that time were also small, in fact just at subsistence level. Hundreds of young men and women left our area during this period on the emigrant ships, many never to return – and these included boys and girls with whom I played around the village.

By one o'clock in the afternoon business in the fairgreen was completed and it was time for something to eat. There were several "atin'" houses and these only operated on special days. The dinners consisted of roast beef, mashed potatoes, peas and gravy, followed by a cup of tea and a paris bun. Some men just bought a few buns or a square of gingerbread and devoured them in some quiet corner and there were others who just drank porter and got drunk.

John James, the local auctioneer, often held an auction on the village street of surplus furniture, carts, traps, harness and farm implements. This event was advertised by Frandie, the town crier who walked up and down the street about an hour before the auction ringing a bell and shouting, 'Auction at three o'clock on the street, a good dresser and an ass's cart for sale; pots; pans; pos and basins as well'.

In the afternoon and evening the pubs were packed with people, for the fair day was a time for renewing old friendships over a few drinks and discussing the day's business. Men who weren't accustomed to drink, often took too much and were eager to fight. When a fight began, others were quick to take sides which resulted in a free-for-all. The local police were usually reinforced for a fair day and were ready to deal with disturbances. The next court day saw many sorry faces leaving the courthouse after being fined a half-crown each.

The favourite drink was Guinness stout. Beer was not so popular except during the summer when Caffrey's Ale was the favourite. Some of the old diehards drank draught Guinness which came in wooden barrels and was 'tapped' by the publican. The whiskey consumed was Irish; Scotch wasn't so popular, although many didn't know the difference. One particular pub in the village sold cheap South African wine known locally as red biddy which was popular because it provided a cheap method of getting drunk. Singing in the pub was frowned upon, in fact it was a sure way of being put out.

With the outbreak of the Second World War the Enniskillen area was packed with troops and the mountains around Derrygonnelly were used as a training area. Coastal Command had a seaplane base on Lough Erne and the giant planes were seen flying low over the village daily on their way to the Atlantic in search of submarines.

Food was strictly rationed, and smuggling of bacon, ham, sugar, clothes and tobacco from south of the border was rife. People set out nightly from Derrygonnelly to Kiltyclogher on smuggling expeditions. It was a risky business and many were caught and heavily fined.

Food rationing was a nightmare for the grocery shops. Butter, bacon, tea, sugar, lard and animal feed were strictly rationed and farmers were compelled by law to plough a large part of their arable land. There were continuous arguments as to the definition of the word 'arable'.

The land around Derrygonnelly was rather wet and shallow and not at all suitable for the growing of cereals or root crops on a large scale. Ministry of Agriculture inspectors arrived to increase food production in the area, but their idea of arable land and the local farmers' ideas were wide apart. However, they had the weight of the law behind them and there was a war on so the farmers were forced to comply and do as the inspectors said. How were they going to plough all this land? They didn't have ploughs for one thing, so many of them set off to Tyrone and Armagh to purchase them second hand. The Tyrone and Armagh men saw them coming and used the opportunity to sell them old obsolete implements. Our horses were not accustomed to ploughing since they didn't know how to walk the furrow. The farmers themselves had no experience of the work. The land was wet and sticky and the whole situation was a recipe for disaster. It was a waste of time and seed but the inspectors stuck to their guns right to the end of the war.

However, farmers received a much better price for their produce; wages went up accordingly and the standard of life in and around our village took a turn for the better.

Doagh Lake, Derrygonnelly.

11 Escape from the Village

THERE WERE TIMES when a young boy just wanted to get away from the hustle and bustle of the shop and yard, from the rattle and jangling of horses and carts on the street. It is difficult for a city or town dweller to imagine such activity taking place in a remote Fermanagh village, but it did!

I was lucky because there were places where I could go outside the village, for a few days at a time, especially during the school holidays. I had a maiden aunt who lived on a small farm at Cashel, about two miles from the village. She was our Aunt Katie and she spent most of her life housekeeping for her old bachelor uncle, my great uncle, Christie. Uncle Christie was around ninety years old and was born just before the Great Famine. To describe Uncle Christie as odd would be putting it mildly: he was an eccentric. In his younger days in the village, he ran the family business, which he inherited from his father, who founded it in 1829.

According to my aunt he was the first person in the village to own a bicycle, a penny farthing. He decided, after purchasing it, to have a few practice runs in the back yard before venturing on to the village street; so he climbed up while the maid held it. When she released it, away went Christie down the yard with gathering speed until he came to an abrupt halt in the river! Some years later, on a more modern bicycle, he cycled on Lough Erne when it was frozen, from Blaney to Enniskillen and back – a distance of about fifteen miles. The following day he performed the same feat on skates. He was a keep-fit addict and for many years he bathed in the Sillees river every morning, winter and summer, followed by physical exercises in his room. No wonder he lived until he was ninety-five.

Often the old timers of the village regaled me with stories

about my great Uncle Christie; all the stories ended up with the remark 'He was an odd man'.

He holidayed regularly on the Continent, sometimes to ski and sometimes to visit the South of France. Just imagine a small shopkeeper from Derrygonnelly, over a hundred years ago, going off to ski in Austria or Switzerland, but Christie did and I doubt if any have done it since.

I heard so many stories about the man that when I arrived to spend a few days with my aunt I made sure that I steered clear of Uncle Christie; looking back, I don't know why, for he was a harmless, pleasant gentleman and anyway at ninety years of age, what could he do? All conversation in the house was conducted in a whisper and I tip-toed past his bedroom door on my way to bed. He never entered the kitchen; so the winter evenings were spent whispering to each other around the hearth fire, while he read in the sitting room. Eventually the old man became bed-ridden and during my visits I was invited to his bedside to chat and sing to him. He was very musical, an expert pianist and seemed to appreciate my singing of children's hymns and songs. He died in 1937 and so passed away a family character much talked about by the older generation to this day.

My aunt took over the little farm and my father leased it from her so I could now stop at Cashel without whispering. I spent many happy days here in peace and tranquillity. I wandered over the hills which looked out to Blackslee mountain to the west and Lower Lough Erne, studded with its little islands, to the north. I still remember, and savour, the tasty meals cooked on the hearth fire and sitting around the fire at night chatting in the lamplight. I never heard her utter an angry word; she was a very Christian, generous, tolerant person who spoke with wisdom on many subjects and encouraged me to express my views. She read the Bible to me and explained and interpreted many important passages. Looking back, I see how significant good conversation is to children and she was a great influence on a growing boy.

Waking up in the morning, the first thing that struck me was the quietness compared to the village; all I could hear was the rustle of the leaves on the trees outside my bedroom window, the hens clucking around the farmyard, the rooster crowing and the old white cow roaring occasionally as she waited to be milked.

There were many chores to be done, for Aunt Katie was getting on in years and quite stiff. I tended the vegetable garden, fetched water from the well, gathered and cleaned the eggs with baking soda, brought in turf and stacked it in the corner beside the hearth, fed the hens and searched around the hedgerows in case any were 'laying away'. Occasionally I milked the old white cow and fed the calf and when there was nothing to be done, I wandered off, lost in thought.

I had two elder brothers: Ernie, who was fourteen years older, helped run the grocery business, while Harry, who was ten years older, was more inclined towards farming. When Harry was twenty years old he decided he had had enough of village life and purchased a hill farm at the back of beyond in the townland of Blackslee.

My father helped to set him up and then left him to his own devices. It was three miles from the village to the lane entrance and another two miles along a rough hilly lane to the farm dwelling. To me it was a heavenly place; the farmhouse must have been at least three hundred years old, thatched and whitewashed. We could sit at the table having our meals and look across a green valley and further on, the broadest part of Lower Lough Erne. To the rear of the house stretched the 'Sour Hill' and beyond, Blackslee mountain, which was a series of heather covered hills and little green valleys containing streams of pure spring water.

I could visit Cashel at any time as I was only a short distance from school but my visits to Blackslee were confined to the holidays or weekends. There were no females in the household so I usually got the job of cook during my visits, supervised by the servant man, Owen.

There were places like Uscenbillagh (the stream of the watercress), garnascilla (the sally garden), the craft field, the dod, the tongue and Christie's knowe. There were fairies at the foot of the craft field and at the dod, and a ghost at the Milltown along the lane. The two horses were released into a field one evening after a hard days work and next morning their tails and manes were plaited so tight that they could scarcely be unravelled; the work of the fairies! Everywhere I

wandered I had the feeling I was being watched and how I
longed to see a fairy, but none ever appeared. Over the next
hill lay Poulafook (the hollow of the Puca or wee people); so
you see our ancestors, who named the place, were convinced
that fairies dwelt in this area. One morning the horses were
found in the field in a lather of sweat, much too tired to work.
'Them damned fairies were riding them around the fields all
night', was the comment.

Once I was travelling along the lane towards the farmstead
when I met an old-timer who had lived in the area all his life, as
had his family for generations. 'Do you see that lane that you
are walking along?' he said, 'That lane was once the main
highway from Dublin to Ballyshannon'. 'Many armies
marched along where you are standing now, coaches drawn
by four or maybe six horses galloped along it, carrying passengers and the mail'. 'Many young people travelled along it on
their way to embark on an emigrant sailing ship from Ballyshannon bound for America, never to see this country again'.
'Aye, many a lonesome tear was shed along that road just
where we are now'. The lane is very seldom used now, most of
it is covered with bushes and grass. It is difficult to imagine
that it was once an important highway. That old man never
read a book in his life so his information, which was correct in
every detail, must have been handed down by word of mouth
during the intervening one hundred and forty years.

Although Blackslee was at the 'back of beyond', it was a
mecca for many young men who seemed to congregate there
at weekends. George and Jack, who previously lived in the
area, came from Derrygonnelly; Danny and Paddy from the
next townland, Percy and Robert from Churchhill, Tommy,
known as Suet, and many others. What was the attraction,
what drew all these young people to such a remote place? Was
it the peace and beauty and tranquillity of the place, was it the
absence of the female of the species or did some ghost, puck or
spirit beckon us? Owen, the hired man, couldn't stand the
solitude of the place; so after his six months hiring was up, he
left and his place was taken by a happy go lucky young man,
Billy.

Some of the visitors stayed overnight and slept in the loft
just under the thatch. The upstairs compartment of the dwell-

ing was known as the loft and we had to be careful not to pop our heads too high otherwise we were speared by the sharp scollops or rods holding down the thatch. Some years later, during the war, Billy was killed serving with the Irish Guards in France, Percy was killed in Burma and Jack was severely wounded and decorated for bravery while serving with the Inniskillings in Italy.

After the weekend most of the visitors disappeared but Jack, George and myself remained if we were off school. Every night we went ceilidhing somewhere. Our favourite was the house of a brother and sister, John and Ann, who lived in a little thatched cabin situated on the crest of a hill in the next townland. They were herds; in other words they looked after the farm and stock for a nearby large farmer in return for the little house, the milk of a cow and the grass for a calf. Ann kept some laying hens and John got the odd day's work during the spring and summer.There were dozens of families in the area who eked out a living by being herds.

Ann had only been to Derrygonnelly three times in her life and those were for the twelfth of July celebrations. She went to Enniskillen once and vowed that she would never go back because the unmannerly people there would not speak to her. She got the name of speaking her mind especially if young girls and boys were good-looking or bad-looking. I remember her telling one young man who had slightly protruding teeth that he had teeth that could rip sacks. This young man was known by the nick-name 'Rip' for the rest of his life. Another young man, who had slightly protruding eyes, was told that he had eyes like bubbles on a piss pot. A young girl in Derrygonnelly was under the impression that she was the best looking female in the district; so my sister persuaded her to visit Ann one summer's evening. Harry, Jack and I accompanied them to Ann's little house where the unsuspecting girl was closely scrutinised. Eventually Jack enquired, 'What do you think of the young girl Ann?', 'Isn't she good looking?'. Ann hesitated a few moments and then proclaimed 'I don't know who you are, miss, but you'll have trouble getting a man for you're like the divil himself'. I'm sure this didn't help the girl's morale; I always thought she was quite pretty.

Ann made the strongest tea I ever tasted. It stuck to the side of the big pint mugs but I enjoyed it immensely. In fact, I could never tolerate weak tea ever since. She was a very good singer and sang some beautiful old songs: my favourite was *The maid of the sweet brown knowe*.

Some nights we went ceilidhing to the home of Danny and Paddy. Their mother was a beautiful singer and she taught many of us how to dance while Danny played the accordion. There were nights when we all sat around the hearth fire singing the old Irish songs and locally composed ballads which are long since forgotten. On moonlight nights we struck out in the opposite direction over the mountain to the White Rocks where there were several ceilidhing houses where we were served tea and fadge bread. Here again there was singing, dancing and story telling. Telling convincing, harmless lies was also a common pastime, and another attraction was a few good looking girls in the area.

There were three female cats in the Blackslee which regularly produced litters of kittens on the high bench of hay in the hayshed. When the kittens were big enough they climbed down and every day after milking they were fed with milk in little pans in the byre. There was an occasion when we found ourselves with seventeen cats of various sizes and something drastic had to be done. One evening after milking, while they were having their meal of milk, we closed the byre door and after much chasing, scratching and spitting, we had twelve young cats in three sacks. As soon as it was dark we set off to the nearby hamlet of Churchhill which contained around nine families and a small shop, a church and a clergyman's residence. We knew that the residents of Churchhill were great cat lovers so when no-one was looking we emptied the three sacks and promptly disappeared into the darkness. I believe their descendents are still in Churchhill to this day and beautiful creatures they are.

During the summer months the young cattle grazed on the mountain and my favourite chore was setting off early in the morning to inspect and count them. They could be anywhere on the acres and acres of mountain, but I didn't mind because I was in another world up there.

I lay in the heather watching and listened to the larks as they soared above me singing their hearts out. I watched a litter of young foxes playing in the morning sunshine watched over by the old vixen and a hare scuttling along a little green valley between the heathery hillocks or a grouse rising from the heather almost at my feet.

When the cattle were inspected, I returned for a welcome breakfast of home-cured bacon and fried eggs, fadge bread and strong tea.

Right on top of the mountain was Blackslee bog where all the householders of the area cut their turf. It was a long uphill drag to the bog but it was worth it for it contained good black turf which was almost as good as coal. My job in the bog was cooking. I gathered some dry turf and lit a fire, then collected water from a nearby spring or boghole and soon the kettle, hung from an iron hook, was boiling for the tea. The strong tea was accompanied by home-made bread, which we became experts at baking, and also boiled eggs. This menu was dished up three times a day and the eggs were usually boiled hard. Three or four days of eating hard boiled eggs, three times daily, often resulted in severe bouts of constipation. However, we soon returned to a menu of oily fat bacon and cabbage and our digestive juices returned to normal.

Both Blackslee and Cashel, indeed most of the houses where we ceilidhed, had crickets in their hearths. These were insects like large grasshoppers and the sound they made was cheerful. You were never alone when you had a cricket for company. Where have they all gone?

The 1930s was a period when many cattle were smuggled from the Irish Free State into Northern Ireland and lots of money was made and lost at this practice. It was a risky business for the smuggler, since he could lose a drove of cattle and worse still, if he were caught himself, he received a hefty jail sentence. On several occasions, when out inspecting the cattle on the mountain, I discovered a number that weren't ours and clearly didn't belong to our neighbours. It was obvious that they were smuggled and it was the custom to hear nothing, see nothing and say nothing and they disappeared as mysteriously as they came. Sometimes a smuggling drover or two arrived at the farm, where they were given a meal followed by a few hours sleep in the loft. They then set off again as quietly as they arrived leaving me with two half crowns on the table; this was a huge amount of money in those days.

Records of the area tell us that there was a school in Blackslee in the early 1800s to facilitate the local children and those from the surrounding townlands so that there must have been a sizeable population in those days. Today there is not a living soul in those houses were we had so much enjoyment and laughter. Some are in ruins, others have disappeared completely underneath the coniferous trees of the Forestry Division. The mountain where I lay in the heather and the bog where we cut the turf are all covered with trees. Some years later I spent a short leave from the army in the Murree Hills which are in the foothills of the Himalayas. Although there was no heather, the atmosphere, peace and the beauty reminded me of Blackslee over six thousand miles away.

Old Willie worked with our family for years with my aunt or my father. He didn't work every day but just when he felt like it and he didn't take life very seriously. I followed him around, for he was one of those people who were willing to converse with a small boy. Some of the conversations were quite sensible, wise and helpful, but at times his imagination ran away with him and he told me about all the ghosts and fairies that he not only saw but talked to, what they said to him and what he said to them!

Willie hadn't a turf bank of his own, so he cut his turf in discarded banks that were almost cut out. The landlord, who owned the bog, decided to open a main drain along one side in order to let away the surplus water. In doing so he left a narrow strip of bog containing about an acre and a half on the other side of this drain. Willie spotted this spare strip of land and decided to take possession and reclaim it. He levelled the rough areas, planted plots of potatoes and after a few years he had a long strip of green meadow land of which he was very proud, for this was his own, the only property he ever possessed. In order to stamp his authority on the little meadow he decided to erect a house on it, which he would build himself in his spare time. He didn't draw plans; he didn't even peg it out, he simply dug a shallow foundation and began to build. His plan was in his mind; it was going to consist of a kitchen and one bedroom, a window in the kitchen, a window in the bedroom, a hearth fireplace, a front door and thatched roof. The stone walls would be held together by lime mortar.

There was one big snag, a supply of building stones. He hadn't the money to buy stones from a quarry nor were there any stones in the nearby bog, so he struck on a long-term plan. He travelled to work each day in his ass and cart and anywhere he saw a few suitable stones he loaded them into the cart. I also kept my eyes peeled and if I saw a few decent stones, I informed him. It was a slow procedure but Willie wasn't in any great hurry.

Every Sunday after dinner I made my way to Tonagh bog to see what progress was being made. Willie was not a tradesman, he wasn't even handy; he never used a horizontal or plumb line; the walls went in and out all over the place, but they stood. I thought that the building of the hearth and chimney might prove difficult, for such a slipshod stone mason, but he managed it successfully.

I don't remember how long it took to build the walls of the little house but eventually it was ready for the roof timber. Here again Willie didn't bother the hardware merchant, for he had the timber collected over a period of time. The surrounding bog abounded with bog oak which was timber buried in the bog for maybe a thousand years. If a length was too long he split it down the middle and these were the couples. These were crossed with lengths of sallies. Thick heathery sods were cut and placed on the timbers and the roof was then ready for the thatch. Old doors and windows were salvaged here and there and the building was complete. Old sacks were ripped flat, secured to the roof timbers and white-washed; indeed the whole building was whitewashed inside and out. The front door and windows were painted signal red and Willie was ready to move in.

Over a period of time two little lean-to sheds were erected at each gable, one for the hens and the ass, the other for turf. A little vegetable garden was fenced off in front of the house and with the purchase of a goat for milk, Willie was as self-sufficient as he was ever going to be. The whole operation fascinated me and how I envied his independence. He reminded me of Robinson Crusoe. I vowed that when I grew up, I would build myself a little house in the bog and keep an ass and a goat.

The Marquess and Marchioness of Ely attending a bazaar in aid of local bands, at the Orange Hall c. 1932. (Lily Dundas)

12   Entertainment

THERE WERE NO CINEMAS in our area when I was growing up. I
believe there were silent films followed by 'talkies' in the
Townhall in Enniskillen but that was another world as far as
the people of Derrygonnelly were concerned. By and large the
people made their own entertainment such as ceilidhing, card
playing, and listening to the gramophone, and dances were
held in country houses with the neighbours invited. There
were two halls in the village, the Orange Hall and the Parochial
Hall and every winter, dances and concerts were held in each.
The concert programmes consisted entirely of local talent, one
act and three act plays, always comedies; together with singing, reciting, dancing and children's items. The halls were
always packed to the rafters. An enterprising lady erected a
large corrugated iron hall and often hired it out to travelling
players such as the Courtneys with their circus and Clarrie
Hayden who was well known throughout Ireland. Here again
these shows attracted large crowds and were of a fairly high
standard. Once a travelling show came to this hall and showed
a silent film called the 'Devil Horse'. Large crowds turned up
as few people in the community had ever seen a film. Different
episodes of the film were shown each night together with a
cartoon. Everyone looked forward to see what the Devil Horse
was going to get up to next and his antics were the main topic
of conversation.

Lord Loftus, who lived at Ely Lodge five miles away, had a
jazz band and played in many of the local halls. He knew not to
play jazz when he performed in Derrygonnelly especially at a
dance. It was not our kind of music so he stuck to the old
traditional tunes; in fact jazz was often banned in some of the
little country halls. His Lordship was also an amateur magician

and I remember him pulling rabbits and oranges out of a hat much to the amazement of us all. He also dabbled in photography and then graduated to making films of scenes and activities around Lough Erne. On one occasion he showed one of his films in the local hall and for many of us this was our first experience of a movie film. As usual the children sat on forms in the front of the hall just a few feet from the screen. We were thoroughly enjoying our first taste of the movie world when the scene changed to a shot of Lough Erne on a stormy day. As the large waves came sweeping to the shore we all jumped from our seats and made for the door for we were sure we were going to drown.

Once a year an Orange soirée was held in the Orange Hall. The evening's entertainment began with the local Orange bands playing up the village street. This procedure was known as 'batin' the town'. The children of the village loved walking after a band imitating the drummers or fluters. Then the crowd filed into the hall and soon every seat was occupied, including the windowsills, with standing room only at the back and down the side aisle. The first item on the programme was the serving of tea and slices of currant loaf. It was amazing the amount of currant loaf some people could eat: they must have purposely fasted for two days so that they could consume their money's worth. When they could eat no more they then dipped the crusts in their cup of tea and threw them at each other. For some reason, anyone with a bald head was a prime target. When the tea was over and law and order restored, the next part of the programme commenced. This consisted of songs, recitations and musical items by the locals including the school children. The highlight of the evening was a fiery speech from a visiting politician, the contents of which were aimed at the shortcomings of the Irish Free State and its leaders.

I remember sitting beside my father listening to one of these speeches. As it progressed, the speaker's face grew red and he sweated profusely; little blobs of frothy spit accumulated at the sides of his mouth. 'You all know the song, *Come back Paddy Reilly to Ballyjamesduff*', he bellowed, 'But Paddy Reilly has no intention of coming back to Ballyjamesduff, and you know why? because there's damn all in Ballyjamesduff for Paddy

Reilly to come back to'. This was greeted with thunderous applause. Nothing much has changed since!

When the programme came to an end it was time for the vote of thanks. This was proposed by the District Master, who probably spent a fortnight rehearsing it, and it was to be seconded by his deputy. At the last minute it was discovered that the deputy was up in one of the village pubs so another member, Robert, was called upon without any warning, to second the vote of thanks. Robert was sitting with his wife in the third row. He was small of stature while his wife was a fairly large woman with a broad 'beam end'. He struggled, petrified, to his feet and exclaimed – 'Ladies and gentlemen, this is the first time I was ever on my feet; but I thank ye all from the bottom of my heart and my wife's bottom also'. Robert received the best applause of the evening.

The Orange band paraded on the twelfth of July, the twelfth of August, the Orange soirée and church parades. The local catholic bands paraded on St Patrick's Day, the fifteenth of August and the odd Sunday, at Bundoran during the summer. Unfortunately St Patrick's Day falls at the time of year when the weather is often cold and wet and often our great patron saint's day is just a damp squib. I have celebrated St Patrick's Day in different parts of the world with great enthusiasm and national pride but in many places at home it is little different from any other day. It's a pity some historical researcher couldn't come up with the discovery that St Patrick's Day should be the seventeenth of June when the weather is better: it would benefit the tourist trade by millions of pounds.

The bands in the 1930s were pretty amateurish, mostly flute and drum bands. These were cheap to establish, run and transport as the bandsmen carried their flutes in their inside pockets. It was quite easy to play simple tunes on a flute and the drummers invented their rhythm as they went along while the big drummer hit as hard as he could as long as his stamina lasted.

Occasionally the twelfth of July was held in the village and was welcomed by all creeds and classes since it brought both excitement and trade and was treated as a festival. The pubs and confectionery shops did a roaring trade.

Garrison band was the first to arrive in the village on the

twelfth morning and after they 'bate the town' they then 'put up' at Dinny's pub. They were closely followed by Whealt, also a flute band and they 'put up' at O'Grady's pub. The members of the Derrygonnelly band were to be found hanging around the Bond Store Bar. The members of these three bands were generally fond of the booze. Few members of Churchhill Silver Band, Tabaugh Pipe Band or Monea Flute Band frequented the pubs, as the majority of their members were teetotal; those who did, used Joe Roger's which had the name of being more sophisticated than the others.

Around twelve thirty the band members and Orangemen made their way to the many 'atin' houses' where they consumed plates of cooked ham, bread, butter and tea. These temporary restaurants were set up in sheds and meal stores and the tables were made of planks on trestles; the seats were also planks on egg boxes so one had to be very careful in case a splinter penetrated the posterior.

The parade of bands, banners and Orangemen, set off from the assembly point and marched through the village watched by large crowds of all creeds from the surrounding area. The Twelfth was a day for meeting friends and renewing old acquaintances. Many a man first met his wife at the Twelfth and introductions were arranged with a bit of matchmaking in view. Lots of 'courtin'' also took place for the grass was long and dry during the month of July and a favourite haunt was the old graveyard.

The playing of traditional Irish music has prospered in the area for generations, especially amongst particular families. Many of them reached a very high standard and frequently performed on the radio. The flute, fiddle and melodeon were the main instruments used in the 1930s and many of the tunes played were either handed down or picked up from the gramophone. The traditional musician was in great demand for the country dances, ceilidhs and dances in the local halls and schools.

Other entertainments were pitch and toss at the cross roads on Sunday afternoons and card playing at night. The servant boys and girls went out ceilidhing most nights and no matter where they went they were served a mug of tea and a slice of bread or fadge. Many of the householders were quite poor and

thoughtous visiting neighbours houses at night for chat + fun + tea could ill-afford these refreshments night after night. Nevertheless no visitor ever left without something to eat. In order to recoup this expense many of the poorer householders ran an annual gamble. All the local servant boys and neighbours were invited to the gamble where they played the card game 'twenty-five'. The entrance fee was a shilling, which included tea, served twice, and the prize was a goose or a pair of cock chickens. At the end of the night there was a small profit and this covered the tea and bread for ceilidhers for the next year.

Pony racing was very popular all over the country during the 1930s and several people in our area were great supporters of this sport. Some bred the ponies while others raced them.

These animals were never kept solely for racing, they did their share of work on the farm and in many cases the pony was the only working animal on the farm. I remember a small farmer who owned a good racing animal which was used daily for hauling the milk to the creamery: it was then hitched to the trap and driven maybe to races in Kesh or Irvinestown. There it was saddled up, raced and in the late evening driven home again.

Occasionally racing was held in a large field beside the village where ponies arrived from all over the County. A few bookies were present, tea and buns were sold, a bar set up, numerous side shows operated and good fun was had by all. One local enthusiast had four racing ponies, Princess of Erne, Sonny Boy, Wide Awake and Fast Asleep.

The Silver Jubilee of King George V took place in May 1935. The children of the village knew very little about royalty. London was in these days very far away. Nevertheless we were all thrilled when we learned that we were going to have a holiday from school on Jubilee Day. We were even more excited when our assistant teacher announced that she was going to organise a fancy dress parade, followed by a picnic and sports. The local bands were turning out and they were going to lead our fancy dress parade up the village street.

We children got together in order to decide, with the help of our parents and teacher, what we were going to dress up as. My sister Elsie and her friend Vivienne dressed as bride and groom; the bride wore a white dress with a long white curtain as a train which was carried by two smaller children. Ada procured an ass and cart, filled it with small dirty little children holding up a placard which read 'The Gypsies have come to town'. Charlie borrowed John's old ass and decorated it with all colours of ribbons; he was supposed to be a clown. Other children were dressed as biblical characters, fairies and animals.

The day before the parade, George and I found ourselves out of things. We were omitted, ignored and forgotten – what were we going to do? 'We'll get an ass too', said George 'and we'll dress up as two runaway slaves'; we had just been reading about slaves at school. We borrowed an ass from 'wee' Georgie and early on Jubilee morning we decorated it with coloured ribbons and rags. We blackened our faces with burnt cork and soon we were ready. We both had red hair which didn't seem to match the black faces.

I mounted the ass Jackie, and George led him by a halter and we joined the parade. Charlie, on his ass, led the parade, followed by the bride and groom, then came Ada and her gypsies and behind them the two red-headed runaway slaves with Jackie the ass. George and I were just nine years old at the time and there were a few matters we overlooked, in our innocence. We didn't realise that Jackie was appropriately named because he was a 'Jack ass'.

The parade moved off, the bands began to play and when Jackie heard the bagpipes he began to roar and at the same time sensed the presence of the female ass in front. He went completely out of control demonstrating his obvious virility: the sweat poured down our faces and mixed with the burnt cork, as we struggled with the love sick animal. He ignored Ada's ass and ploughed through the bride's train as it wound around his feet on his way towards Charlie's ass at the front. The crowd on the sidewalk cheered heartily. I never dreamt we could be so popular. Just at the last minute two men rushed from the crowd and rescued the situation by spiriting the frustrated animal away to the stable. George and I were mortified and I'm sure some of the ladies in the crowd turned their reddened faces the other way; how were we going to face our teacher. Wee Georgie, the owner, commented 'It must have been them confounded bagpipes that upset Jackie'.

Sligo Grammar School hockey team, 1941. The author is third from the end of the back row on the right.

13 Growing Away

IN 1938 my father and my teacher must have held a conference regarding my future education; I did not know, since I was not consulted in any way. My eldest brother would probably take over the business. My other brother was already farming so I suppose my father thought that I was a budding doctor or a clergyman, maybe even a bishop. Just imagine a bishop in the family!

It was finally decided, with no consultation whatsoever with me, that I was to become a boarder at Sligo Grammar School, provided I passed the scholarship examination; otherwise my father couldn't afford the fees. The master took me in hand and he was a lot more determined than I was that I should pass the exam. He put me at a desk by myself and crammed me from head to toe with Irish history, geography, arithmetic, English and the two old faithfuls, scripture and English grammar. I parsed, analysed and declined for hours on end. Eventually I did the exam, scraped a scholarship and my fate was sealed. I suppose my parents thought that they had a genius for a son but I soon learned that they were wrong.

A large envelope arrived from the headmaster of the school containing all the details of fees, extra expenses and a long list of items which would be required, such as shoes, suits, shirts, sheets, overcoats and so on. My father and I went to Belfast in the lorry to purchase the clothes I would wear on Sundays – a black jacket and waistcoat, black striped trousers, white shirts, Eton collars, black tie and navy blue overcoat. I fitted it all on when I arrived home and when I looked in the mirror I felt an awful idiot and hoped that none of the other boys in the village would ever see me. I was bewildered by all the fuss for I had never been away from home before so I didn't know what was in front of me. This was all to the good, otherwise I might have rebelled and refused to go.

The big day arrived. My trunk was packed and put on the back of the lorry. I bid a pathetic good-bye to my family and the staff who were standing on the sidepath outside the shop. Many of the inhabitants of the village stood in their doorways to give me a wave and wish me luck. The entire community knew that this was the fateful hour; it wasn't every day that someone from their midst went off to boarding school.

I climbed into the cab of the lorry and off we set, Harry the driver and I, to the railway station at Enniskillen where he set me in a carriage on the train bound for Sligo town on the old Sligo–Leitrim line. I had travelled once before by train to Belfast so this was only my second experience of this mode of transport.

I duly arrived in Sligo, but where was the Grammar School? I hadn't a clue and there was no-one to meet me. Nowadays young boys going to a boarding school for the first time are accompanied by their parents who help them unpack and settle in, but it wasn't done those days. I stood outside the railway station with my trunk in complete bewilderment and then I spied an old fellow with an ass and cart who looked as if he was a hawker or a rag and bone man. I approached him and asked 'How much will you charge me to bring the trunk to the grammar school', not admitting that I didn't know where it was. 'A shilling', was the reply; so we lifted the trunk into the cart and he set off while I followed at a discreet distance as I didn't want to be seen arriving at a boarding school in the company of an ass and cart. Just imagine, a boy arriving at Eton or Harrow in this manner; if they had done, no doubt they would have called this noble animal a 'donkey'.

I was shown upstairs to a dormitory where all the new boys were to sleep. It held twenty beds but there were no cup-boards, bedside tables, or any individual privacy whatsoever. We had a linen bag tied to the leg of our bed for our dirty clothes and when we undressed for bed we folded our clothes and hung them around the bed as best we could. On the landing outside the dormitory each boy had a peg for his suits and a shelf for the remainder of his clothing.

The bathroom served not only twenty boys of our dormitory

but ten more who slept in an adjoining one. The bathroom had one toilet, two baths, two urinals and four wash-hand basins.

Our daily lives were ruled by a large bell. It rang at seven thirty at which time we got out of bed and queued up for the use of the wash-hand basins, urinals and toilet. We dressed quickly and assembled at five minutes to eight in a large classroom where we were inspected by the duty master for cleanliness.

Breakfast was a plate of porridge followed by a cup of tea and a slice of bread and margarine. Dinner consisted of two courses and was quite good. We had meat, vegetables and potatoes followed by a sweet. At six o'clock we were served tea, bread and margarine. Twice weekly we got jam, once weekly a boiled egg and once a week two sausages. For supper we were served the left over heels of bread and a cup of milk. The margarine was slightly melted and then painted on the bread with a brush. In all my time at the school I never saw a boy leave food uneaten on his plate. It's a good thing the school didn't keep a dog or pig to eat the leftovers. They would have died of hunger. Before I went to boarding school there were certain foods I wouldn't eat but all that changed very quickly for once there, I ate anything that resembled food.

The first night in the dormitory was a traumatic experience for the new boys. We were all suffering from loneliness and frustration. Many cried. I felt so bad that I couldn't cry. Then suddenly in the darkness we were taken, one by one, to the bathroom where we were stripped naked and plunged into a bath of cold water. When we struggled out of the bath we returned towards our beds amidst a flurry of whacks on our bare bums with bedroom slippers. This was our initiation.

Things couldn't possibly get worse. They could only get better but not much. For the first year the new boy was bullied by the older boys. He cleaned shoes, football boots and sports kit and was responsible for keeping all the floors clean.

Parents were not encouraged to visit the school during term or send food parcels and there were no mid-term breaks. Once we said goodbye to our families at the beginning of term, that was it until the end. We received one shilling a week pocket money. One penny went on the collection plate at morning service on Sunday, one penny for evening service, two pence for a stamp when writing home and the remainder we spent at a tuck shop on Sunday afternoons.

Two afternoons a week we played rugby; one afternoon hockey and on the others we either went walking in line, two abreast under the supervision of the duty master or we just hung around the school and, although playing cards was strictly forbidden, we played whist.

There was an asylum in Sligo for the mentally ill and whenever we had a rugby match against another school a large contingent from this institution arrived to support our school. They knew absolutely nothing about the game but they gave such ardent support that they were worth ten points to our team before the game commenced. The opposing team were mesmerised when they saw these enthusiastic supporters running up and down the touch line in their big hob-nailed boots. The only drawback was when the ball was kicked into touch and they all raced to retrieve it and fought for possession. On Sunday afternoons when we were out walking in line under a master's supervision we often met about forty inmates also walking in line under the supervision of a warden. We were going along a quiet country road for a walk whilst they were going to watch Sligo Rovers play. That was the year the great Dixie Dean played for them.

There were around sixty boarders and twenty day boys at the school and the staff consisted of the headmaster, six teachers and a matron. The headmaster kept himself aloof from the boys, was a stickler for discipline and, I suppose, did his best on a meagre budget. I found all the teachers quite good considering the conditions in which they taught and the lack of facilities. The matron was responsible for the kitchens, dormitories, food, laundry and of course our health and welfare. She was known to generations of boys as 'bitchie', a name she didn't deserve in my opinion.

If you didn't feel well you went to see the matron during break-time from prep. It didn't matter if you had a pain in your leg, your stomach or head, she treated them all the same, with a glass of foul-tasting liquid known to us all as 'black jack'. I don't know what it contained but we certainly visited the toilet more often. She was also an expert at squeezing boils and that about sums up her medical ability.

The school had a close association with the Church of Ireland and this resulted in religious instruction being taken very seriously. We learned hundreds of Bible verses off by heart, together with the catechism, the Thirty-Nine Articles, morning service, evening service, communion service and many collects. We had morning and evening prayers, went to church twice every Sunday, choir practice twice a week and, when old enough, Holy Communion, every other Sunday. Some might say that so much scripture and church going was unnecessary, maybe they are correct but ever since, even when I was thousands of miles from Ireland, I always made a point of attending a place of worship regularly no matter what the denomination.

What seemed like the longest period of time in my life was the first term at boarding school. I thought the Christmas holidays would never come and how I longed to see my family and friends in Derrygonnelly.

After my first holiday at home I settled down and took things pretty well in my stride.

I was always reasonably good at sport and found it easy to make friends but academically I was nothing special. As time went on I found myself struggling with the languages – French, Latin and Irish.

After three years at this seat of learning. I was transferred to Portora Royal School at Enniskillen, as my father's health deteriorated and he subsequently died leaving my mother living alone. I became a day boy at the school which was very different from boarding. It meant that I cycled ten miles to the school every morning, in all weathers, leaving home before eight o'clock and returning the ten miles in the evening, often after darkness if I was involved in after school activities. This was during the early years of the war when petrol was severely rationed resulting in a very restricted bus service.

No matter what part of the world you visit sooner or later you will meet someone who was educated at Portora, and more often than not, in a position of authority or importance. Both my father and grandfather attended the school and I was extremely proud to be part of such an illustrious establishment. In spite of this I never liked the school and although it was much better equipped than Sligo, in my opinion the teachers were not as good or as dedicated. However, I must not blame the school or the teachers for my lack of ability for during my second and third year at the school I didn't work hard enough and as time went on lost interest in school work. This was a period of my life when the supervision and advice of a father would have been very beneficial.

The headmaster was a large energetic man with a voice like a sergeant major and had a mop of red hair. He had been an Irish international and British Lions rugby forward. The school, after an absence of thirty three years had won the Ulster Schools Cup two years running and were firm favourites to do so again. After only three weeks at the school I was very proud, at just the age of fifteen, to find myself a member of the 1st XV. The team had had quite a good season and managed to reach the final again against RBAI (Belfast 'Inst'). The game resulted in a draw. Forty six years have passed and the school has not reached the final since. I was given an Ulster trial in 1944 but alas I just managed to make the substitutes bench. This was the year the great Jack Kyle made his debut in representative rugby and he went on to be the best half back the world has ever seen. Many members of those three great teams served in the forces during the war and some paid the supreme sacrifice. I remember playing for my Battalion team in Hong Kong when six of its members were old Portorians.

My housemaster 'Mickie' taught Latin and was also the rugby master. He accosted me regularly saying 'Parke, you are useless at Latin but you could be a really good rugby player if only you would cease smoking'.

Because these were the war years and clothes were strictly rationed, it wasn't compulsory to wear school uniform. Once I pinched a very loud red neck-tie belonging to my elder brother and wore it to school. Like my headmaster I also had a good mop of red hair. One morning at prayers the headmaster mounted the prayer desk to announce the opening hymn. He suddenly stopped in mid-sentence and stared down the assembly hall at me. He then strode down, with his gown flowing behind to where I was sitting and in front of the five hundred other boys bellowed 'Stand up Parke'. I quickly rose to my feet while he stared in horror at my red tie. He then bellowed 'Parke! People with our colour of hair should not wear red ties, take it off at once'. I took the flashy tie off, put it in my pocket and I never wore a red tie since.

There were many boys and girls who cycled home from the various schools in Enniskillen and needless to say quite a lot of horseplay took place along the road. This was a time when many of the boys and girls experienced their first kiss and cuddle; some might say that it was part of our education. I did not even know the names of all the girls and I still meet the odd one after all these years when I receive a strange shy stare and they probably say to themselves, 'you were an amateur'.

With all the distractions it eventually dawned on me, as I'm sure it had possibly already dawned on my teachers, that I hadn't a hope of passing the Senior Certificate Examination. I left school a complete academic failure. The only success I had was on the sports field and that was no asset to a future career, so I took what I thought was the easy way out, boarded the train for Omagh and joined the Army.

After the ceremony of 'swearing in', I was given a travel warrant and ordered to my army depot in the south of England in order to complete my recruit training. A farewell dance was held for me in the local hall and off I set on the train for Belfast and then to Larne where I boarded the boat for Stranraer.

These ships crossed the Channel in pairs so that one could help the other if torpedoed. They zig-zagged all the way across in order that submarines would not have enough time to aim. Both ships were packed with civilian and service personnel and I spent a cold, uncomfortable night on the deck because there wasn't a square foot of spare space below. The sea was extremely rough and as this was my first experience of travelling on board a ship, how I wished I was back in Derrygonnelly.

After that miserable crossing I spent many hours travelling in a crowded train towards my depot in the south of England. It was during this journey that I witnessed the devastation and destruction caused by German bombs to the towns and cities of England. I arrived at Euston Station as it was growing dark and for a young lad from Fermanagh, London during the blackout was terrifying. The London underground was a new experience, the platforms were packed with people either travelling or settling down for the night using the station platform as air raid shelters. I was relieved when I eventually surfaced at Victoria Station and boarded a train for my final destination.

I and a few other recruits arrived at the barrack gate some time during the night and we were shown to a blanket store where we slept until morning. I was cold, hungry, tired and miserable and if by some magic spell I could have found myself back in my native Fermanagh I would have made sure that I never left.

Early next morning a bugle sounded and in rushed a lance corporal shouting 'outside, outside'. Everything was done 'at a run'. We ran to the washhouse where we washed and shaved in freezing cold water and at long last reached the cookhouse where we were served baked beans swimming around in red liquid, bread and tea. 'Outside, outside' bellowed the lance corporal and we were off to the quartermaster's store where we were issued with ill-fitting uniforms, shirts, boots, socks, long johns, knife, fork, spoon, plate, mug and a rifle and bayonet coated in grease, together with many other pieces of equipment. 'Outside' bellowed the lance corporal again and off we trotted to our allocated barrack room where we left our equipment. Off again to the medical hut where we were ordered to strip off. There we were medically examined and injected several times in both arms with blunt needles. 'Get dressed' and off again to the straw hut where we filled long canvas sacks with straw; these were our mattresses.

We were then introduced to our platoon sergeant and his junior instructors who all spoke with cockney accents. I hadn't a clue what they said and they didn't understand my Fermanagh accent. The sergeant stood on a table and addressed his new intake of recruits. 'Pay attention you scruffy lot of layabouts; my name is Smith; S stands for Smith and S stands for something else and I'm both'. That night I climbed on to my bunk, lay down on my straw mattress, wrapped myself in my army blankets with no sheets or pillow. The bugle sounded 'lights out'. It was then that I realised that I had left my Fermanagh childhood far behind.